1 for Library
1 in master
at least 8 perhaps
2 for display rm, 2 for 1st floor
File-B's Sketches
door to A/C unit
30"
4 1/2'
56"
3) rm beam
4) get dust out of vents in stickly rm
R- 5) clean off dust on A/C table
6) Jorge when returning (did he get latest drawing?)
BB now what - leave plain shelf for now - call!
7) Jimenez - match mahogany color of gym! Its better +
- needs shinier lacquer (where's sample)?
- why no stain on panels, big doors
8) Pablo - remove ball!
9) BP - Wm - how is it possible that neither gift wrap door nor window casing was done in basement?
9A) no samples for corridor?
10) Alan why nothing done more on bedbd?
11) Do people leave when I leave??
Jimenez - round (sand edges of square mahogany in dressing rm -
13) stain above windows (ser. rm) J - Fit in pcs. of wood above between windows
Elias new put casing around gift wrap rm w. rosettes? - Jumbo
together
for loft -
comes from England?
for gift wrap
catalogue??
in screening rm
was wrong + I used it in
simple

My Passion for Design

A Private Tour

VIKING

BARBRA STREISAND

My Passion for Design

Contents

Principal Photography by Barbra Streisand

I'm writing this book to share my love of architecture and design, and to pay homage to those artisans who cared and carved and made things by hand, before industrialization and mass production. In this frenetic world we live in, it seems as if machines are taking over . . . computers that drop the stock market a thousand points in a matter of minutes, metal detectors, oil-drilling robots.

I don't pretend to know much, but I do think that technology without consciousness invites disaster. If only our hearts were as evolved as our minds . . . .

I've always admired originality in any form, and there are certain artists whose personas inform their work and make it immediately recognizable. So I dedicate this book to those who have left us works that have stood the test of time . . . and today's artisans who carry on that tradition.

GARDEN

Introduction

I follow the light.

My bedroom gets that pure, clean light of early morning, and I'll reach for my laptop and papers and work in bed for a while. Here's the real truth . . . Samantha (see cover) has usually fallen asleep at my feet, and I don't want to disturb her. I get a lot done in bed . . . writing . . . reading . . . trading . . . eating. I trade stocks. It's a way of gambling without having to get dressed. My husband usually has tea and fruit for breakfast. I like something a little more substantial . . . pancakes made with spelt or buckwheat flour.

At midday, the sun is dazzling. It makes the ocean shimmer. But I'll look at it through a window because it's too bright. When the sun is directly overhead, it's harsh and damaging. Anyway, it's a good time to be inside, eating lunch.

I prefer the gentler light you get in the late afternoon . . . that mellow, honey-colored light that slants across the floor, like you see in some of Edward Hopper's paintings. Everything looks prettier in that kind of light. And that's the best time to visit my roses, after 4 o'clock, when they're backlit. I have to get my camera so I can capture them in their glory.

Sometimes at the very end of the day, if I have time, I'll sit for a moment on a hidden bench in the garden that gets the last warmth of the sun.

Natural light is the most beautiful to me. When I was trying to persuade a studio to let me make *Yentl*—the story of a girl who masquerades as a boy in order to educate herself—I went to Czechoslovakia and shot a little eight-minute film in natural light to show them my concept. Every country has its own particular light, and in Czechoslovakia it was very soft.

I also feel passionate about color. I used to have long discussions with my gardener, when we were choosing flowers, about what is red and what is pink. You can't just say something is red. What kind of red is it? Does it have blue in it? Or orange? Does it have a faded, timeworn quality, like the red you see in a Rembrandt painting? There's a moment in *Yentl* when she touches the prayer shawl, before she sings the first song, and I wanted the velvet slipcase for the shawl to be Rembrandt red. It's a very specific shade.

I've never liked bright primary colors. . .except for pure lipstick red. They lack complexity. I don't like royal blue but I've always loved that French blue-gray. I don't like yellow . . . unless it's the color of sweet butter . . . with a little honey in it. I stay away from orange (too in-your-face). I love

PREVIOUS PAGES: *This is my own version of a barn, combined with elements of a New England farmhouse. The front is barn red and looks like Connecticut . . . the back is off-white and looks like Nantucket . . . because I love both.*

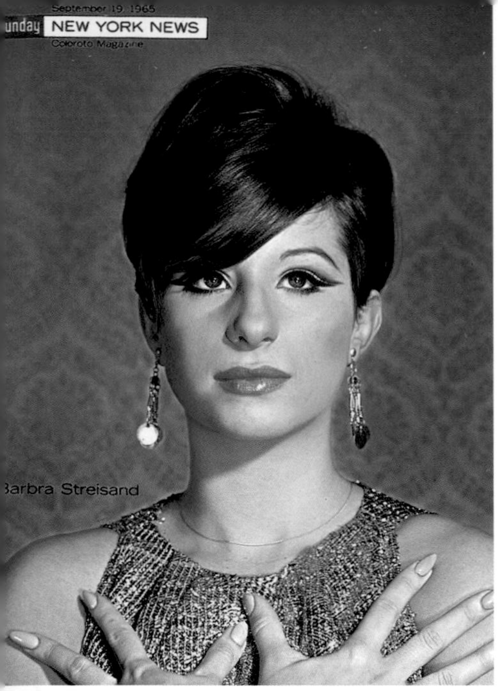
September 19, 1965
NEW YORK NEWS
Coloroto Magazine
Barbra Streisand

LOOK
35 CENTS · APRIL 5, 1966
GENERAL RIDGWAY
condemns "all-out war" in Vietnam
CATHOLIC EDUCATION'S TIME BOMB
The crisis that led to revolt
at St. John's University
could overturn the entire system
BARBRA STREISAND
The not-so-funny story
of that Funny Girl

ARCHITECTURAL DIGEST
THE INTERNATIONAL MAGAZINE OF FINE INTERIOR DESIGN

My whole life, in a sense, has been a search for beauty.

various shades of pink, but I'd have to say my favorite color is burgundy. Maybe it's because my mind flashes back to a burgundy sweater with wooden buttons that Toby Borokow knitted for me when I was five years old. She took care of me after school while my mother worked. I was anemic, and one summer I was sent off to a health camp where they put us in starched royal blue uniforms. The only thing that set me apart was that burgundy sweater.

I also have intense relationships with furniture . . . probably because we practically had none when I was growing up. After my father died at the age of 35, when I was 15 months old, we moved in with my grandparents, who had a little apartment on Pulaski Street in Brooklyn. I slept in a bed with my mother, and my brother had a rollaway cot in the same room. We didn't have a couch . . . I guess because we didn't have a living room. I played under the dining table. I liked it under there. It felt safe. When I was eight, my mother remarried, and we moved to a housing project on Newkirk Avenue and got our first couch. I was thrilled. It was a nubby olive green and gray . . . shiny gray . . . and I loved that ugly couch. My mother kept it covered in plastic. Everything was covered in plastic, including the lampshades. I slept in this living room until I was 13.

It's hard to say how one acquires an eye for art or design, but I don't think I developed it at home . . . unless it was in rebellion from what I was seeing. My mother used to wash the floor and then spread newspapers over it, which I never understood because the print would come off on the floor. The plastic and the newspaper hurt my eyes. When you don't like your surroundings, you have to use your imagination to create a world you do like.

I moved away from home when I was 16. I had this burning desire to be an actress. I shared an apartment with a friend, Susan Dworkowitz aka Lanell, on West 48th Street in Manhattan, next to the acting school where we both took classes, and got a job as a clerk in a

I've been through a lot of different styles in hairdos and clothes and decorating, from my Jacobean four-poster in New York to my 1930s projection room in Los Angeles, from my Art Deco house in Malibu to the rustic American look of old painted furniture. OVERLEAF: *I always thought there should be harmony between the colors of a room and the colors of the clothes you wear in it.*

printing office. We had no money but we needed furniture, and that's when I discovered the thrift shops on Second and Ninth avenues. I found an old dresser and put a fish tank on top of it. It's something to look at that moves. I picked out a fake Persian rug at one of those dubious stores on lower Fifth Avenue. I couldn't afford to buy art, but I found old gilt frames for a few dollars and hung them on the walls, just framing space. I thought that was beautiful.

When I was 19, I got a part in my first Broadway show, *I Can Get It for You Wholesale*. The stage manager told me about a $60 walkup on Third Avenue over Oscar's, a fish restaurant. It was a railroad flat with a bathtub in the kitchen, but I loved it because it was my first apartment on my own. I was dating the show's leading man, Elliott Gould, and after six months he moved in with me. Can you imagine, Elliott is 6'3", and we slept in a single bed, because that was all that could fit into the room.

After we were married, we moved into a duplex at 320 Central Park West, where Lorenz Hart had once lived with his mother. The apartment had six rooms, an elegant staircase, two fireplaces, and a terrace—quite a change from a railroad flat. I decided to do a Victorian living room and had these gorgeous burgundy velvet drapes made, lined in a burgundy and off-white herringbone tweed. There was something so interesting about the juxtaposition of that menswear tweed with the lush velvet. I was 21 years old, but the impulse I had then was the same as I have now . . . to combine opposites. I've always been interested in that dichotomy . . . masculine and feminine . . . simple and elaborate . . . rough and smooth. I was also very practical—the drapes were reversible, so I could use them on either side.

But then my concept changed. My friend Charles Murray used to give me chicken soup and take me shopping. He introduced me to the antiques stores on University Place, which were cluttered with French furniture and porcelain and bronzes. Suddenly I wanted Louis, Louis, Louis—as much as I could find. I went to Versailles and stood in Marie Antoinette's bedroom and was completely seduced by all that delicate embroidery. I came home and decided to do a French living room in beige, dusty rose, and celadon green, based on an Aubusson rug I found (a copy . . . I couldn't afford the real thing). So I moved the burgundy velvet drapes into the den and painted the walls burgundy as well. I had a burgundy velvet couch made and covered two side chairs in that same herringbone wool tweed—that was a little unusual at the

Vaughan/Architectural Digest. Copyright © Condé Nast

Photograph by Howell Conant

I sold my favorite Tiffany lamp at auction during one of my periodic purges. It's the one with a peony shade on a red turtleback mosaic base, and I deeply regret not giving it to a museum where many people could enjoy it . . . and I could still visit it.

time, putting a menswear fabric on a chair. But I loved all those masculine pinstripes and tweeds. I added a grand piano and a Victorian loveseat, which I had upholstered in a burgundy paisley. And then an idea occurred to me. I had some leftover fabric, so I designed a dress to match the loveseat. Why shouldn't you wear clothes to match the room? It seemed perfectly logical to me. Many years later, when I was collecting pieces by one of my favorite architects, Frank Lloyd Wright, I read that he had designed clothing for his clients to wear in his rooms. Of course. I completely understood that.

With the first money I made on Broadway, I began to buy Art Nouveau furniture, like an Emile Gallé cabinet that I saw in Lillian Nassau's shop on E. 57th Street. I had to pay for it in installments and since I had no place to put it, Lillian stored it in her basement for me. I had never seen furniture like this . . . wood carved into liquid curves . . . and then there was the luminous art glass. I fell head over heels for Tiffany lamps . . . Art Nouveau bronzes . . . Vienna Secession pewter. I knew nothing about them, but they were eye candy for me. And their beauty seemed to nourish my soul . . . still does.

Objects were my friends. The skill and creativity that went into making these things beguiled me. Finding them became a challenge. I loved the hunt. For instance, the first Tiffany lamp I ever bought had a peony leaded-glass shade with a glorious red turtleback base and tiny mosaic tiles in the colors of the rainbow. It was the most beautiful thing I'd ever seen. Then I found out Tiffany also made a green and a yellow version, and I had to search for all three. Why? I don't know . . . to celebrate Tiffany's genius . . . to complete the set. I wasn't satisfied until I found them.

I don't like feeling a sense of loss . . . even something I've lost at an auction can haunt me. Years ago, a rare pin by the Viennese architect Josef Hoffmann was coming up for sale, and I left a bid because I couldn't attend. I lost it to the next bidder. (This is why I don't like to leave bids. You have to at least be on the phone.) I was so upset, and then of course I wanted it even more. My dear Renata Buser, who has been my personal assistant for more than 35 years, tried to have the pin copied for me but it wasn't the real thing. I wouldn't give up until I had traced that pin halfway around the globe, to a dealer in Germany. I ended up paying him four times what it went for at auction . . . and then never wore it. Because it wasn't about the pin. Sometimes I think it's all connected to the loss of a parent . . . because you'd do anything to get that mother or father back. But you can't . . . yet with objects, there's a possibility.

I love decorating. Over the course of 30 years my apartment in New York went through various incarnations, from Jacobean and English chintz to Louis XV and then Americana. I had a house on Carolwood Drive in Los Angeles filled with Art Nouveau, until I turned toward the more simple lines of

Arts & Crafts 20 years later. In Malibu I lived on a rustic piece of property we called the ranch and decorated that house with American folk art and old painted furniture and Tiffany lamps. When a dilapidated tract house next door became available—I seem to attract these houses, as you'll find out—I bought it for privacy's sake, thinking it would be easy to add a second story and transform it into an Art Deco house. That turned into a five-year ordeal and by the time it was over, I never wanted to look at Art Deco again.

But the story of all of those houses could fill another book. They'll have to wait for Volume II, because I want to tell you about my latest project . . . an elegant barn.

I've always loved barns. I love American architecture—Colonial houses . . . Federal houses . . . saltbox houses . . . the historic houses of New England. I would go back east during the summer and go antiquing along Route 7 in Connecticut and look at all the old, beautiful farmhouses. My New York apartment was formal, and the house on Carolwood Drive was pretty formal as well. I liked the idea of building a barn where I could just relax.

Then in 1992 when Bill Clinton was elected president, I fell in love with America all over again. I became fascinated with American history, art, and architecture. (Politics, I had always been interested in.) I toured the White House and the State Department and was blown away by the elegance of the rooms and the beauty of the fine 18th-century furniture. I wanted to see more. I visited Monticello and Mount Vernon. I went to the Smithsonian and the National Archives, where I touched the Louisiana Purchase . . . or was it the Monroe Doctrine? (I get them confused.) At the Library of Congress, when they asked if I wanted to look at my own things, I said no. I just wanted to see Thomas Jefferson's drawings of the dome at Monticello.

I spent two days at Winterthur, the extraordinary museum of American decorative arts in Delaware, and it was eye opening. I

The lamp in the middle was my first and favorite Tiffany lamp, with its superb peony shade on a red turtleback base. The red is the rarest of the three. I've never seen another like it . . . or like any of these. The top lamp has a dragonfly shade on a green turtleback base. The one on the left has yellow roses on a yellow turtleback base.

wanted to learn more about 18th-century American antiques. In 1993, when I was preparing to return to the stage for my first concert tour in 27 years, I looked at the set that was being designed, which was very modern, and remembered the tearoom at Monticello, where everything was off-white, with sheer curtains and graceful arched windows and busts of famous men on the wall. I told them that was the environment I wanted to sing in ... be in. That, to me, was elegant.

And then somehow that vision of 18th-century elegance merged with the barn idea. I thought, How do I put these opposing elements together? How can I combine Federal architecture and fine mahogany furniture with my love of rustic barns and simple painted furniture? I didn't know yet how they would go together, but instinctively I knew they could.

This is somehow related to directing films. It's very exciting to start with an idea and make it come alive with actors and sets. It uses everything you know or have ever experienced. It's the same with building a house.

What is it that you imagine? How do you manifest that? That's the challenge ... that's the fun ... that's the horror!

It's interesting that two films I really wanted to direct, *Yentl* and *The Prince of Tides*, were very difficult to get financed, but eventually they got made. Years later I ran up against the same obstacle on another film I felt passionate about. Only this time it failed to come to fruition. I had to redirect that energy into another passion . . . my passion for design.

So this is my elegant barn. Instead of directing a movie, I built a house.

Thomas Jefferson's Monticello (TOP AND BOTTOM) *inspired the set for my 1994 concert tour* (MIDDLE AND OPPOSITE). *I don't call myself a designer. I certainly don't design for other people, although I may give them a little advice, if they ask for it. I don't charge. I just see things in my head, whether it's a stage set or an album cover or the rooms in my house. I'm told I have a good eye. Maybe that's because I'm a nitpicker. (This is not a good trait.) But things have to look a certain way. If they're out of place, it makes me feel out of sorts.*

Monticello/Thomas Jefferson Foundation, Inc and the photographer Laurence Bartone; Concert Photographs by Kevin Mazur

An Elegant Barn . . .

. . . Starts with a Chicken Coop

I love my girls. They give me fresh eggs every morning that are the most beautiful shade of pale green.

I've always wanted chickens. Shouldn't a barn have animals? I wish we had room for cows . . . pigs . . . I love pigs. (I've been collecting miniature figurines of them for years.) But the most I've been able to manage is chickens. We have 22 of them and one rooster. At one point, I decided to give him away because he does that crow thing all day long and I thought the neighbors would complain. But the next day I missed him, so I had him picked up and brought back.

Actually, the story of the barn really started with a house I wanted but couldn't have.

I first saw it 1984, when I was living down the road at the ranch on weekends and at my Carolwood house during the week. I never really liked the Carolwood house, even though I lived there for 30 years. Initially I had rented it while I was doing *On a Clear Day You Can See Forever* and when I went back to New York, I didn't know what to do with all my things . . . furniture, clothes . . . you know, *stuff.* So I bought it. (The rent was applied to the purchase price, and it was a good investment.) It was Mediterranean architecture . . . red tile roof, stucco walls . . . like you see everywhere out here . . . and I'm not a big fan of Mediterranean architecture unless it's in the Mediterranean. Although the house did have some lovely characteristics, which I will explore in Volume II . . . if I ever get around to it.

But when I looked out the windows of that house, I saw only the trunks of the trees. I longed for a piece of sky. Besides, my bedroom was on the street, with tour buses going by every few minutes announcing my name on a loudspeaker. On Friday nights I would escape to Malibu. But now the ranch, with 24 acres and five houses, was just too big for me. I wanted to downsize . . . sell the ranch, sell the Carolwood house, get rid of the apartment in New York . . . and just have one house on the ocean. That's when a broker showed me this other house for sale. From the outside, it was not great. Gray wood siding like some modern contraption. But the inside had a rustic charm. My good friend Cis Corman and Renata loved

I try to give my Araucana chickens (free range, of course) a good home. They lay green eggs and this was the very first one. The 1930s Ford pickup truck was a gift from my husband. Metal pigs are better than no pigs. PREVIOUS PAGES: *Different rooflines suggest different time frames.*

it. But my boyfriend at the time thought it was too close to the cliff, and my business manager told me I couldn't afford it until I sold the ranch. (Eventually I gave it to the state of California as a conservancy center.) And it would have meant another construction project, which was not a happy thought since I was exhausted after spending five years building the Deco house. So I didn't buy it.

I was so forlorn when I found out that it was sold to someone else and they had already started renovating it. After hours, when the workers had left, I would climb over the fence and walk around to see what they were doing and pine, literally pine, for this house that I didn't buy. I loved that it was on a cul-de-sac. I loved the view. The couple who bought it knew how much I liked it, and three years later offered it to me for more than four times what they had paid for it. I countered with three times what they had paid, which I thought was reasonable, but they turned me down. So I lost it again.

Seven years later, another piece of property on the cul-de-sac became available, and I tell you, it was the ugliest house I've ever seen, a one-story tract house from the 1950s with rocks on the roof. But I bought it, because it was *near* the house I loved. (There was only one house between them.) And I thought, Well, I'll knock this horrible house down and build the American barn I've been dreaming about for so long. Meanwhile, I became friendly with the couple who lived in the house in the middle. They were in their 90s and very sweet, and I would go and talk with them. When they decided to move up north they sold it to me. So now I had two houses—both so run-down that neither was livable—and I thought, Okay, I'll knock them both down, make one house on the two acres. (Each property was an acre.) Then guess what happened? The couple in the house I loved got divorced, reduced the price, and I was finally able to buy it . . . the only one I really wanted in the first place.

It's now my main house, and I adore it. Why? Because I didn't have to build it! I didn't have to pick out the hardware and the crown moldings. Years of my life were spent on moldings . . . casings . . . baseboards. Details, details, details . . .

And we might as well get one thing out of the way right now. There may be more details about paneling and paint in this book than you ever could have imagined or ever wanted to know. If you don't want to read about it, I understand. Just look at the pictures. But I was obsessed. You have to understand something. I *love* details. As the architect Mies van der Rohe once said, "God is in the details."

Of course, you could also turn that around and say the Devil is in the details.

For me, it's another one of those dichotomies . . . because both statements are true.

Here you can see how the new buildings are situated, starting with the chicken coop on the left, then the mill house on the pond, and then the barn. This picture was taken way before the roses had grown over the trellises.

Building a Dream

For some people, building a house is a wonderful experience, but that's not how I would describe it. I really enjoy the creativity of the design phase. But to actually have to build it? Did you ever see the movie *Mr. Blandings Builds His Dream House*? Or the remake, *The Money Pit*? It's one problem after another, which I learned firsthand from the nightmare of building the Deco house. I think one of the reasons it took so long to get started on the barn is because I was unconsciously putting off the actual construction.

And I really didn't need another house. I had the main house to live in, and I decided the house in the middle would make a great guesthouse. (You'll see what I did with them later.) Building the barn was more about giving shape to an idea. It was an outlet for my creative energy. It took the place of making a film.

Let me tell you, it's much easier to make a film. When I'm directing a movie, I sit down with the production designer and describe the characters and how I imagine each set . . . Biedermeier furniture and oak paneling seemed right for Susan Lowenstein in *The Prince of Tides* . . . and then magically it appears when you need to shoot. Of course, a set has to last for only a few weeks, but still it's amazing. I never had any problem with movie people. We speak the same language. Anything I ask of them, they find a way to do.

So my first instinct was to hire a production designer to help me get my vision down on paper. I did hire two of them, but something always happened . . . they got a film and they disappeared. Then I decided that it might make more sense to hire a regular architect who was familiar with the Malibu building codes. The first one I tried drew something that looked way too modern. Then I turned to another architect . . . and another . . . looking for someone who could interpret what I was imagining.

You see, there was nothing here when I started. I had demolished the ugly tract house, cleared the land (I had to take down 30 eucalyptus trees that were in the way, but I replanted other trees in other spots), and filled in an empty swimming pool that was an accident waiting to happen. Of course, I then had to redig the hole later when I decided to do a pond.

I had made up a whole script in my head for this house. The idea was that back in 1790 (I had

ABOVE, LEFT: *Here is the original house as I bought it in 1994, with rocks on the roof. I stored antiques in it for seven years, until we demolished it* (ABOVE, RIGHT). *That was an exciting day.*

found an old sign that said 1790) there might have been a mill house on a pond, grinding corn or wheat that was stored in a stone silo. Eventually this fictitious family who owned it built a little farmhouse near the silo. Several generations later, in 1904, a wing was added on either side. I picked 1904 because four is my lucky number... I set *Yentl* in 1904... and I knew all these wonderful architects like Hector Guimard and Charles Rennie Mackintosh and Greene & Greene were alive and practicing then, and I wanted to somehow incorporate their work into the design.

A lot of the old farmhouses I had seen in the course of my research had been added onto over the years, and I liked the idea of different sections with different rooflines. Since I love silos so much, I was going to have one in the front and one in the back. Originally they were both round. Then one day Jim and I were driving up north, and I happened to spot an octagonal silo made with clapboard. And I said, That's it! That's the shape it should be in the back. An octagon made out of wood. Maybe shingles...

The design process seemed to go sooooooo slowly. The first architect would appear for a meeting and then come back three weeks later having forgotten the changes he was supposed to have made. After that experience, I had another architect move in with me for five days a week so I could keep an eye on what he was drawing. (He lived too far away to commute.) A third architect couldn't hold back his yawns if a discussion lasted more than two hours. I'm sure I wore them all out. And I found that most architects on the West Coast weren't that familiar with Eastern architecture. They weren't particularly interested in what barns looked like back in 1790 or 1904. That's why I ended up going back to my movie people. They enjoy doing research. They do period films all the time.

If I could ever get the barn down on paper, I still needed someone to build it. I couldn't find a contractor. One wanted me to leave for the duration of the construction, another would do it only if I had an owner's rep. Another couldn't start for a while. Finally I hired my brother-in-law, John Johannessen. I hoped he at least would have my best interests at heart. He and his family lived in Orange County, and I moved them up here to begin the work. Time was running out on the permit, and we had to start building without a complete set of plans.

This is not something I recommend. I did have a core set of drawings by this time, with all the structural and mechanical specifications, but the interiors hardly included any details. I just didn't want to spend any more time waiting for drawings. I thought we could figure it out as we went along. Big mistake.

But if you look at this situation with a more positive frame of mind, you could also turn it around and say that it allowed us to be more creative. Something special happens when you are in the moment ... in the reality. I could look at a room as the walls were going up and say, Wait a minute. That really should be an arch. As some people have told me, they doubt it would have turned out to be as interesting if everything had been worked out beforehand. Who knows?

After we got our building permit in 1999, we were told that the house had to be moved back 15 feet. Why? I wanted to build on the original footprint, and it took three more years before the city agreed. But that was just the first of many problems ... like those huge HVAC units. The last architect had nine of them, a major eyesore, as you were approaching the house. I had to hire another contractor to help John figure out how to eliminate some and move the others.

ABOVE: *This very big hole will eventually be the foundation.* BELOW: *The framing gives shape to the basement rooms. That large space in the foreground will eventually be Jim's workshop.* OPPOSITE: *Now you can start to see the composition of forms on the front façade.*

We finally finished the construction and the landscaping in 2008, and until that time I was constantly in building mode, even when Jim and I were supposedly on vacation. For two summers in a row, we took a 10-day boat trip from Sag Harbor up to Maine, stopping along the way in various ports. We would get off the boat and go into town to visit the historic houses and do some antiquing. I kept stopping the car to photograph details and measure things, like the clapboard on some old house we were passing. Was it four inches wide? Four and one-eighth inches? Four and a quarter? Then I would e-mail the pictures back home to the construction crew and ask them to make a mockup and e-mail me a picture so I could decide what would look best on the barn.

Someone told me about a man in Connecticut named Harold Cole who dealt in old wood. Then while I was doing an interview with Diane Sawyer and telling her that I was going to build a barn, she mentioned that her husband, Mike Nichols, knew *the* old-wood expert and that she would get me his name. I told her to send it along with her recipe for cornbread. (When I was at their house for dinner, she made the best cornbread with real corn and gave me some in a bag to take home.) I wanted that recipe, and when it came, with the name, wouldn't you know it was the same Harold Cole? So he was my source for old wood, and I even brought him to L.A. to show my carpenters how to nail up the paneling like they did in the old days, so that the wood could expand and contract.

I hired Jack Taylor, a wonderful art director, to draw up a few rooms with specific details. What was kind of shocking is that even with all the measurements, it could still go wrong . . . sometimes because somebody decided to change things without asking me.

I bought the American eagle weathervane, which dates back to 1860, years before I broke ground on the house. Here the clapboard is painted with just the white primer coat, and the stone silo looks too prominent. It will blend in much better against the barn red.

I think the colors of the plants should relate to the colors of the house. Coleus is the perfect burgundy. John Petritz, my pond man, even found burgundy water irises.

Room for Improvement

I used to wince when I was called a perfectionist. The word seemed to have a negative tone to it. What's wrong with being one anyway? It means you strive for excellence. You want something to be the best it can be. To please the public, you first have to please yourself, and you are your own toughest critic. It's a curse and a blessing... more of a curse. And there are many times you have to compromise, but that can lead to creativity... if you can turn a disadvantage into an advantage. Ultimately there is no such thing as perfection. When I was 15, I wrote in my journal, "Perfection is imperfection." There has to be some sort of flaw to keep it human. At this point in my life, when people call me a perfectionist, I think, Why fight it? Just take it as a compliment. ❧

My voice was hoarse from shouting over buzz saws for years. And now there are certain phrases that make me crazy, like "We're working on it." What does that mean? It means it's not done. In fact, it's far from being done. What it usually means is they haven't even started it yet.

And waterproofing. That's another word that makes me cringe. I went for an expensive waterproofing system in the barn, with copper sheeting in between the interior and exterior walls. Then a guy comes to install the alarm system. Nobody says to him, "Wait. Don't do anything until the contractor gets here." In 45 minutes he drilled right through the copper. He ruined 30 windows . . . and my waterproofing contract.

Let me say this: It was not an easy project. It was a creative challenge to blend several styles from several centuries. Some architects told me to not even try. But that was my dream, my vision . . . very similar to making a film. As an actress, I have always relied on my intuition. Same thing here. I saw the house in my head and I thought it would work.

I'm happy with the results... even though I don't live in it. But actually, I never planned to. I love where I live now, in my main house. Building the barn was like completing an art project. I don't watch my movies after I make them. I don't listen to my records after I record them. So why would I live in the house that I built? The creative process is over for me. It's done.

And now I'd like to share it with you.

OPPOSITE: *The house is simple black and white on the façade that faces the ocean. I used the rough side of the clapboard here and the smooth side on the barn-red façade in front . . . I like the different textures. Black and white is such a great background for one more color . . . like the vibrant lavender of this rosea iceplant.* ABOVE: *And here's the view from those black rattan chaises.*

THE MILL HOUSE

When I was planning my new house, I knew the back would have an extraordinary view of the ocean. But what could we do with the front?

In 1989, I was antiquing in Vermont and bought a hooked rug with a picture of a mill house and a waterwheel. I kept it in the garage for the longest time and then one day I looked at it again and said, That's it! A waterwheel! We'll build a mill house with a pond. The wheel will turn and make ripples in the pond, and we'll have movement and water on both sides of the barn. It would give much more interest to the street side of the property.

OPPOSITE: *The rope to my right is attached to a pulley up top, and would have been used to hoist up the bales of hay. I love what the wavy glass in the door does to the reflection.*

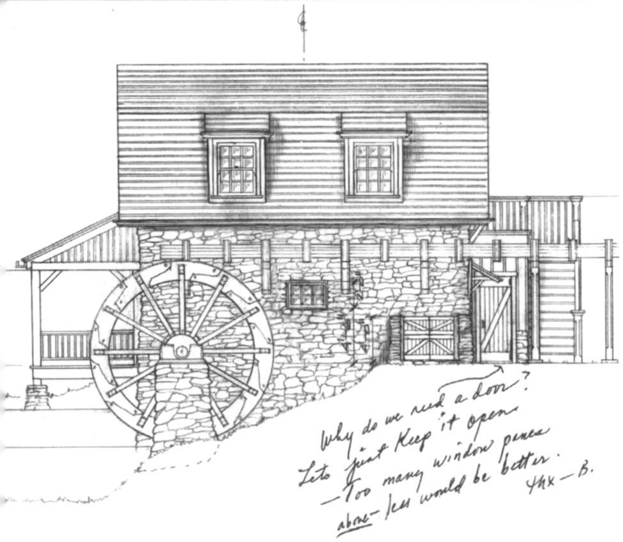

Let me just say this now: It is by no means easy to build a pond. The first people made it too small and lined it with rubber alone, which turns out not to be allowed. We had to rip it out and start all over again with heavy rebar to conform to code.

Since the new house was going to be an elegant barn, the mill house was an opportunity to be more rustic . . . rougher and cruder. I had looked at so many barns over the years that I could already see it in my head. I wanted Xs on the doors and a gambrel roof. But what about the waterwheel? How do you build that?

You can look up waterwheels on the Internet, but they're made out of metal nowadays. And then Jim and I took a trip up north in our pickup truck. (We need the truck so we can bring home any antiques we find along the way.) He took me to a place called the Apple Farm in San Luis Obispo for homemade ice cream. And there it was—this amazing old wooden waterwheel, just what I wanted.

Jim happens to be a part owner of a lumberyard in San Luis Obispo. His partner, Nick Fortune, was able to track down the man who had originally helped build that waterwheel. He was eighty-eight years old and gave them advice on where to find parts. Nick also managed to locate three very old books on waterwheel theory. It was a blessing to have Jim and Nick figuring this all out, especially after I had become completely frustrated with various architects. (One drew the wheel way too small, one had it too far away from the mill house, and another had it on the wrong side altogether.) This elderly engineer knew all about fulcrums and scuppers and pressure and power. And you'd better know what you're doing when you're building something like this. Jim loved working on the project.

Our wheel weighs 4,000 pounds and stands 14 feet high. Its main spokes were cut from hand-felled white oak (the kind used in

LEFT, FROM TOP: *Here's the original rug that sparked the idea. I colored in the production designer's sketch—at this point the porch had a tin roof, but that had to go in order to conform to code. The model was very helpful when we were trying to work out proportions. On the waterwheel side, the mill house has a stone wall—more impervious to splashes.* OPPOSITE: *I actually prefer the latticed porch now. It filters the light and creates such interesting shadows. When I was visiting Jim while he was making a movie in Canada, we saw a stone bridge that gave us the idea of how ours should look.*

One summer, when I got together with my dear friends Evelyn Ostin and Joanne Segel, we sat on this porch and looked out at the water and reminisced. We've known one another for a very long time. We shared our innermost thoughts and feelings here. It's a meditative spot.

Sunday on the pond with Jim. He gave me the boat . . . perfect size, perfect color. See my koi? I'm such a color nut. Even the fish are only black or white. No orange. (A little yellow is okay.) I love water lilies.

ship frames, so it could stand up to water) and trucked here from Kentucky. But guess what happened along the way? Would you believe the truck was hijacked? We had to wait for them to make a whole new set.

I never thought this would be so complicated. And then came the flume! (That's the chute that drops the water onto the wheel.) I thought the rafters that stick out from the mill house and hold it were too long, so I had them cut down. Then they were too short. Oops, my mistake. And for some reason they were already sagging, even without the weight of the water. So we had to extend the wood

ABOVE: *Eventually, the mill house will be our garage. After the doors were framed, I didn't like the plain rectangular shape and decided to give it a little more pizzazz* (OPPOSITE, TOP). FAR LEFT: *The beams in here are 200 years old and very crude—gray, splintery, and full of holes . . . just what I wanted.* LEFT: *The walls have layers of stone at the bottom, as if the plaster that covered them had crumbled away over the years.*

and then wrap it with iron straps to hide the joint. Don't even ask about the waterproofing . . . .

Nothing was easy. When we were building the mill house itself, we couldn't find enough vintage red barn siding to cover the whole thing. But I did manage to locate a few old boards, and I knew my movie people could match the color and texture of their faded red paint, worn away in places so the old wood showed through. They started with new cedar siding and first had to paint it brown to add depth to the color. Then they had to age it. I'm told that movie painters used to put bits of cotton in

FAR LEFT: *The dormer windows originally were drawn too wide, too modern, but now they have the right proportions. I used old-fashioned wavy glass for the panes. At first I was thinking of doing a tin roof, but when they set out the samples it looked too shabby. I ended up going with multicolored slate* (ABOVE) *reclaimed from old roofs in Vermont.* LEFT: *Here's a painter, trying to match the vintage red siding on the right.*

the paint—it's called roping—to give it that clumpy look, especially in the corners. But now they have new thicker paints to duplicate that texture. You get a weathered effect instantly.

In retrospect, we made a big mistake. We should have painted black over the white Tyvek paper that wraps the insulation, so when the boards shrink in colder weather you wouldn't see the white underneath. I had to have my guys paint every gap black with a tiny brush. But I love that about wood, that it contracts and expands. It's a living thing.

When people first see the mill house, I usually get one of two reactions. Some people say, "Wow! Where did you find this old barn?" They assume I had it moved here from back east. And others look at it and say, "Are you going to take down that old barn now?" I *think* that's a compliment.

ABOVE: *We're in the process of building the supports in preparation for the wheel.* RIGHT: *Here it comes, all the way from San Luis Obispo. The highway patrol had to issue permits for bridge clearances, which were down to inches on a couple of the overpasses.* OPPOSITE: *A huge crane picked the wheel up from the truck on the street and then had to lift it over the trees, and the mill house, to set it in place.*

$ 8800

Thank god, everyone measured correctly and it slid right in, just where it was supposed to be.

The Storm Cellar

I wanted a storm cellar, like in *The Wizard of Oz*. It's not that I'm expecting a tornado, but with climate change, you never know! One architect drew a 16-foot-long cellar. I looked at this concrete block thing, and it didn't look like any storm cellar I'd ever seen. They were usually 6 to 8 feet long, according to my memory. "Why do you need sixteen feet?" The answer: "Because it's code, and you have to have a certain ceiling height as a man walks down the steps." Hmmm. So how did Auntie Em and Uncle Henry get down there with only 8 feet?

I said, "I don't buy it. First, it can't be more than eight feet. It won't look right. We have to find another way."

I'm a person who does not believe in the word no.

There *has* to be an alternative. But here's where they get you: When somebody tells you that this is the way it has to be and they're professionals, you tend to believe them . . . at first. But I have found out the hard way that you must question everything.

In fact, I've always been accused of questioning too much. Actually, it's a very Talmudic thing to do, to question everything . . . sometimes even the answer is another question. A 16-foot storm cellar did not seem logical to me, and I just couldn't give up searching for a solution. And we found one. We lowered the floor and made the steps go farther into the basement, which now holds all our pool and pond equipment. One contractor wanted to install a push-button electric system to open the doors. It was Jim's suggestion to do it more naturally, with pulleys and sandbags. Even he's surprised it works! ❧

They used to paint advertisements on the sides of barns. Here's one for Beech-Nut gum . . . slightly modified, because we live at the beach.

The Design Room

We built the mill house first so we could use it as a design studio. We moved in big tables, computers, all my reference books, and binders filled with photographs I had taken over the years, with this project in mind. We had catalogues for everything from moldings to light fixtures to hardware. Normally all that stuff would be in an architect's or an interior designer's office, but this was a very hands-on project. All the decisions were made here.

I always had an assistant devoted to this project, and at least one draftsman on site every day, so any idea I had could be drawn. I liked the immediacy of working this way. Once I saw it on paper, I could decide whether it was worth developing. I didn't start out planning to do so much myself, but every time I tried to hire an architect or a designer it didn't work out. My ideas were too specific. And good designers have their own ideas and don't want to be expediters. Besides, they were usually juggling several jobs and couldn't work fast enough for me. ❧

ABOVE: *This was command central during the construction process.* OPPOSITE, ABOVE: *On one of our trips up north, Jim and I were looking for old farm implements when I spotted some antique cabinets in a shop. We bought all nine (they were made of oak and came from a haberdashery store) and filled them with samples of hardware and all sorts of materials. The flat files hold drawings.* OPPOSITE, BELOW: *We created storyboards for each room with photographs of the furniture I planned to use and swatches of fabrics, trimmings, paint, and wallpaper.* OVERLEAF: *Here's a glimpse of some of the elements involved in building this project. This was the fun part.*

REET / ROOT CELLAR
RT NOUVEAU / DISPLAY ROOM
RESSING ROO

JACQUELINE'S
VINE
(SILO BATH)
4 DOUBLE
ROLLS

KNOBS

BUNGALOW BASICS LIVING ROOMS
BUNGALOW BASICS BEDROOMS
BUNGALOW BASICS
BUNGALOW BASICS FIREPLACES
WINTERTHUR
AMERICAN HOME
Garrett • Larkin • Webb
BARN
CLASSIC INTERIOR DESIGN
TRIMWORK
ROBERT ALLEN
ROBERT ALLEN
EAST ELEVATION

Library
Root Cellar 339 SF
Basement Bath
Antique Closet

DOOR KNOBS, PULLS, STOPS & ESCUTCHEONS
DRAWER PULLS AND KNOBS

The Lap Pool

The bridge offers a shortcut across the water and masks the wall between the upper, irregular part of the stream and the more rectilinear lap pool. We raised the level of the Jacuzzi in the foreground so you can gaze at the ocean while you relax and let yourself be pummeled by the jets. The planters for the Butterscotch roses are recessed into the bluestone deck, so the whole scene feels more integrated.

I love looking at water. It's like a living painting—always in motion. I find it mesmerizing, meditative, relaxing. I already had the view of the ocean and the pond and thought it would be interesting to continue that theme and direct your attention to something equally beautiful on the side of the house. So I decided to build a lap pool. Now, practically everywhere you look, there's water.

The pool reflects the sky. It sparkles in the sun. You can step out that door on the second floor from the gym and walk down the stairs and have a swim to finish off your exercise. According to the local building code, the pool could be only eight feet wide, so if two people are swimming they have to take turns or watch out that they don't collide. But the Jacuzzi at one end is big and deliciously warm, and when you're lying there, you feel like you never want to move.

The same Pennsylvania bluestone that I used to make the paths through the garden became the deck. The deck ties into the stone façade on the house, and the stone connects the pool to the earth. I had the interior covered in gray plaster because it gives it more depth and darkness. The darker a pool, the more natural it looks.

I wanted the upper part to feel like an extension of the stream, as if it ran underground beneath the path and then emerged again to form this new body of water. So we made that part more rough and raw. You can sit there amid the rocks and let the water flow over your shoulders.

A simple white wooden bridge arches over the spot where the meandering stream transforms into the long rectangle of the pool, and lets you walk straight across to the garden. I drew the bridge. John built it for me. And Vicente Viera, my right-hand man, and Javier Cansino, my gardener, laid out the path in a couple of hours. I would be lost without these two men. Like me, they want to do things fast.

LEFT, FROM TOP: *The excavating machine does its own laps. Laying stone is like fitting together the pieces of a puzzle. The pool is lined with gray cement mixed with sand made from crushed bluestone. The upper part of the pool looks natural—a rough tumble of boulders that turns into a lap pool on the other side of the bridge.* OPPOSITE: *The bridge is constructed of white-painted wood to echo the trim on the barn, the stair railing, and the arbor.*

Stone paths lead you through the garden. I have always been attracted to old stone. And there's something even more beautiful about it when it has moss growing on it.

When you're standing on the second-floor deck outside the gym, those three chaises (BELOW) *give your eye something to focus on. I bought them before we laid out that irregular circle of stone, so I knew exactly how much space I needed.* LEFT: *I wanted the stones in the walkway to look scattered, and we drew out the rough shapes in chalk* (FAR LEFT) *so we could find stones that were similar. We chipped away the edges here and there for a more natural look.*

Everything you see on the grounds was carefully planned to look natural. After the excavation of the basement for the barn, we had several mounds of earth. Instead of having it all carted away, we used it to create a more rustic landscape, with gently rolling hills. At one spot, we needed some steps. One day, I came home and the stonemason had taken out my lovely grass-covered hill and made this thing out of concrete blocks. I was appalled. Why did you destroy my hill? "Well, you need structure under the steps and we have to attach the stones to something."

"I don't buy it," I said. "Absolutely not." I had just come back from a trip through England's Lake District, where there are stone walls going back to the 11th century that are still standing. They didn't even use any mortar! And they certainly didn't have concrete blocks. Anyway, it came out perfectly after I asked them to please put back my hill and make more natural-looking steps.

LEFT: *My heart sank when I saw my gentle hillside cut away to create this cement-block stairway. It was quickly torn out, the hillside was restored, and I had it redone with more organic-looking stone steps* (BELOW).

It Takes Effort to Make Something Look Effortless

We had to plan out every curve in the stream and place every boulder along the banks to make it look as if it had just evolved naturally over the years. Can you imagine making a simple country stream out of concrete and rebar? At first, they made the concrete walls too high, so we had to cut them down—if anything, a stream should be lower, not higher than the ground. And I wanted the fairy-tale sound of a babbling brook, so the water had to tumble over the rocks in a series of waterfalls. But how high should they be? And what about getting across the stream? I thought it would be nice to put flat-topped stones in a rough line so you could just step to the other side. Then we planted some grasses, burgundy daylilies, white iris, and white heliotrope that smells like vanilla. ❧

I had all these images in my head when we were laying out the driveway. I kept thinking back to the English countryside, where we shot some scenes for *Yentl,* and the rural roads of New England. I wanted the driveway to look as if a horse-drawn cart had worn a winding path through the grass, and then cars, coming later, just followed it. The driveway wanders a bit, like the stream, instead of heading directly for the stone bridge in a straight line. I like the way the twists and turns make the property look larger.

LEFT: *We marked out the rambling path of the driveway, filled in the wheel tracks with cement, and then covered it with stones and surrounded it with grass for a rustic look.* BELOW: *As you drive in the gate, I wanted a tree but wasn't sure what size it should be. My landscaper located a Chinese elm that might work and we rigged a pole with an umbrella top so I could get a preview of the height and the spread of the leaves.* OPPOSITE, BELOW: *Here's the after shot, with the Chinese elm in place by the gatehouse.* OPPOSITE, ABOVE: *If you step back toward the gate and look in the other direction, toward the barn, you can see how the elm (now on the right) acts as a foreground piece to the larger composition.*

There are very few straight lines in nature. Every wall we made is a little haphazard. Every path rambles.

In Tune with Nature

A stone path winds all the way from the front gate to the chicken coop and around the mill house to the barn . . . just where you might want to walk. And I wanted it to be bordered by a stone wall—rough, not smooth, with cracks and crevices where plants would seed themselves, and places where tree roots would dislodge some stones. When the stonemasons finished a portion of the wall, it ended in a sharp ninety-degree angle. I looked at it and thought, It's too stiff, too straight, too modern. So I asked Luis, a wonderful stonemason—and person—to take off some stones and round the edges to make it feel more natural. "Make it look as if it's been softened by rain and wind and the passage of time." And he did! ❧

OPPOSITE: *I love the look of stone paths in the rain. If you've ever noticed, almost every street in a movie is wet. They water it down before the shot to make it look better, especially at night . . . it shines, it glistens. It's more photogenic. Here the rain was real. It made my photo look so much prettier.*

The Rose Garden

Look at this Butterscotch rose—a pale gold like something out of an old painting. Or this Lavender Pinocchio—a faded peach color like the sea anemones in my fish tank. Isn't that incredible! These kinds of subtle colors are so amazing to me.

I never had a garden before. I grew up in Brooklyn, in an apartment building surrounded by cement. Even when I moved to Central Park West and had a terrace for the first time, it was not exactly Eden. Anything I put outside was soon covered with a layer of soot.

Now I wake up every morning and see the ocean and the sky. I walk through the garden to see what's bloomed overnight. I have a sign by the path that says "Won't you come into my garden? I would like my roses to see you." I find it unbelievably gratifying to be this close to nature. Every day in the garden is different. The flowers are constantly changing. It keeps me fascinated.

All of this land was overrun with bushes and weeds when I first saw it. We had to clear the junk away to lay out the beds. I decided to make the paths random rather than formal, because I love English gardens. It's hard to grow roses by the ocean because of all the salt. The moist air also encourages mold and rust, and you have to spray the plants often to keep it in check. The first landscaper I hired put the vegetable garden in the middle, with roses all around it. But then every time we sprayed, it would also spray the vegetables. That made no sense. After building the house, we moved the vegetable garden off to its own area, and we spray the roses only when the wind is going in the other direction so the vegetables stay organic.

ABOVE: *When I bought the property, the wishing well was already there, and I kept it because I loved it. We had to replace the wood posts because they were falling apart and we added a little wooden shake roof. Now it's brimming with passionflowers and Butterscotch roses . . . and lit from underneath, so it becomes a little beacon of light at night.*

Lavender Pinocchio

The arbor that leads to the barn is covered with Butterscotch roses. This rose has such an unusual color—a deep mustard with tinges of red when it's in bud and then when it blooms, it becomes a faded gold. It's a color that feels antique . . . old and mellow.

Dan Bifano, my rose expert, is a wonderfully knowledgeable friend who has been with me for many years and has taught me so much about roses. I don't care if they're French or English, hybrid or antique. What matters to me is the color and the scent. Roses come in all sorts of shapes and sizes. Some have ruffly petals, some have flat. Some of them don't even look as if they belong to the same species. The variety is so intriguing. They're like different children from the same family, and each one has its own unique character. Some, like Louise Odier, have been around for more than a century. Louise Odier is an old garden rose with a classic cupped shape—the petals curl in concentric circles, which was highly prized in its day, instead of flexing away from the center like a modern hybrid tea rose. And what about that heady fragrance? Probably the same since 1851, when it was introduced.

Angel Face

Stephen Rulo

There's nothing like an old garden rose. I can't stand the hothouse roses you get from a florist, with those tight-looking heads that hardly ever open and just wilt on the stem. And they have no scent! If a rose has no scent, it better be the best color—like the Ingrid Bergman rose, which is a pure, lipstick red. When Tom Carruth of Weeks Roses asked if he could breed a new rose and name it after me, I said I would be honored. Of course it would have to have a wonderful scent, and the color was very important to me. The Barbra Streisand rose is very healthy and disease resistant. It blooms a lot and it's a bit of a chameleon, like me. It starts its bud in my favorite color—burgundy—and then as it develops it turns from a mauvey dark pink to a pale lavender. One stem could give you up to eight roses—it's very generous.

I grow roses with particular rooms in mind. The pure red roses always go into Grandma's house, where they pick up the color of an old red, white, and blue WPA sign that hangs in there. I love the color red in a rose, but you'll never see me wearing it (except as a character in a movie, like Roz Focker). The dark and light pink roses go into the cream

Violet Mist

It's a miracle to me how roses grow and get their colors. Some bloom for a few weeks, others for only a few days. I've often wondered where the scent comes from. Does it go up from the seed into the stem, mixing with earth and water? Are there little cilia that move it along?

Barbra Streisand

Frederic Mistral

Cape Cod

Louise Odier

Ambridge Rose

Yves Piaget

Rouge Royale

Taboo

Black Magic

In The Mood

Ingrid Bergman

ABOVE: *In the garden, there are arbors and paths and various secret places where nobody can find me. It's a bit like hiding under the table as a child.* OPPOSITE: *I love the wildness of an English garden, with perennial plants that come back year after year like old friends. Because they reseed themselves, they don't always show up quite where you expect them. The wind takes them who knows where.*

living room in the main house, where those colors are used as accents. My bathroom gets all shades of pink and burgundy. The off-white roses go into my off-white bedroom. And the lounge in the barn gets only Butterscotch roses, because that color looks so beautiful against the blue.

There's so much to learn about roses. Dan told me that each rose goes through its own cycle during a day. It will be most fragrant around 11 a.m. (by the way, if you blow on a rose, the warmth of your breath releases more of its scent) and the best time to pick it is around 4 p.m.—but that also depends on the weather. I'll put several different shades and varieties of roses in a vase—a dark red next to a dark pink. If you squint, it all blurs into one color. I don't understand those stores on the street corner, where you see bouquets with one pink, one yellow, one red, one orange, and one purple flower. Not for me, anyway.

There's always so much to do in a rose garden—deadheading, pruning, feeding, mulching, spraying. But the rewards are so lovely. Every day the buds are a little bigger until they burst into bloom. And when one is ready to expire, the one next to it on the same stem is about to open. Birth, death, renewal—you experience the whole cycle of life in a garden.

GARDEN

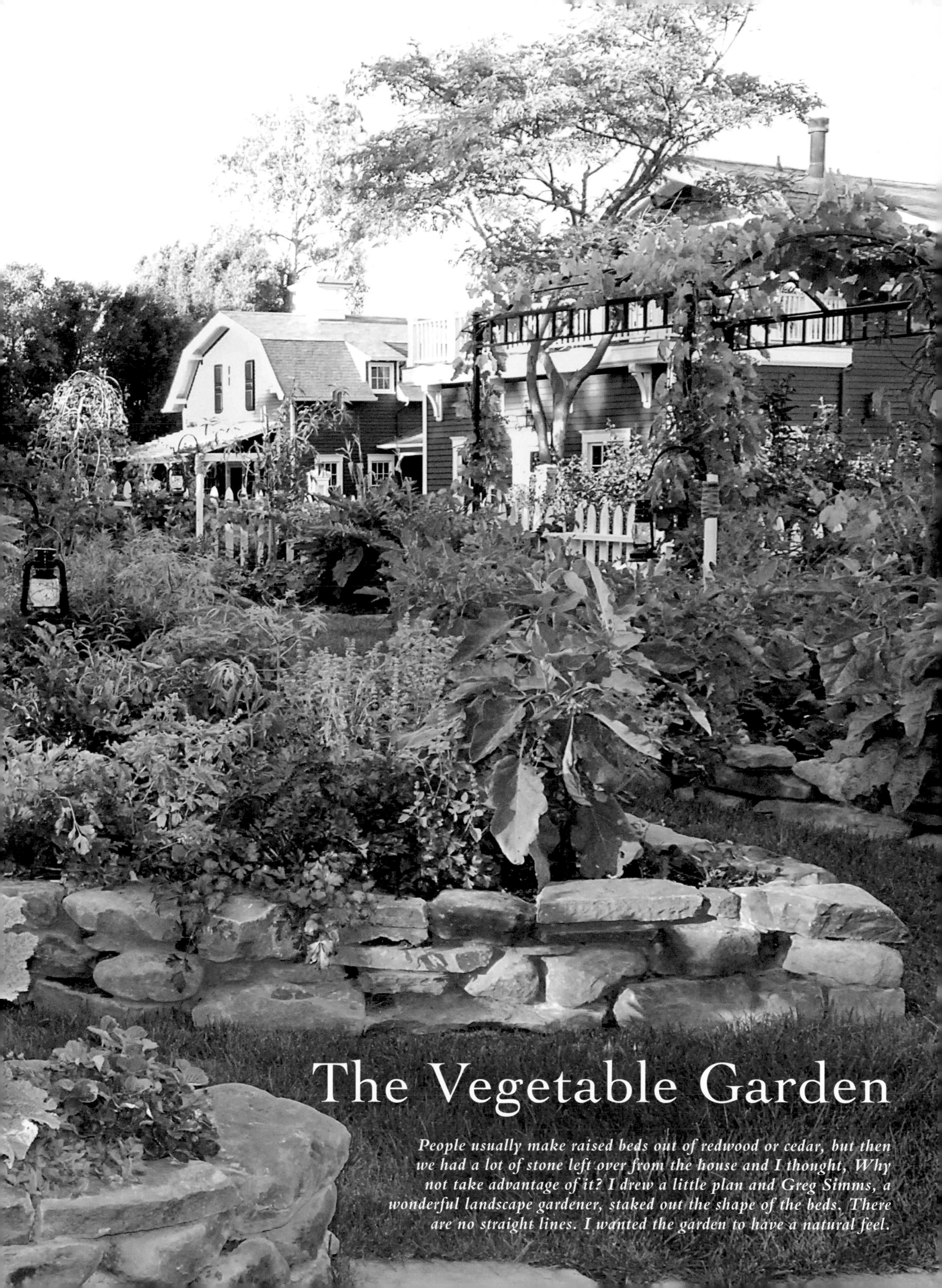

The Vegetable Garden

People usually make raised beds out of redwood or cedar, but then we had a lot of stone left over from the house and I thought, Why not take advantage of it? I drew a little plan and Greg Simms, a wonderful landscape gardener, staked out the shape of the beds. There are no straight lines. I wanted the garden to have a natural feel.

There is nothing like the taste of a plum, still warm from the sun, that you've just picked off a tree. Or raspberries right off the bush—I have to bend down and eat a few every time I pass. Imagine the sweetness of a handful of blueberries that didn't have to ride in a truck. It's so fresh!

Then there are apples and oranges, peaches, grapes, and pomegranates. We even grow *fraises des bois*—wild strawberries. You never find them in grocery stores or restaurants here, but they're everywhere in France during the summer. And last but not least, my favorite—the delicate passion fruit, grown on the fence surrounding the chicken yard. It's a dark, wrinkled, dried-out looking oval on the outside, but inside it is so sweet and tangy and multilayered in taste, and so good for you. It just shows, Never judge a passion fruit by its cover.

We eat out of the garden all year long. A salad made from lettuce and greens like arugula that you've grown yourself is so crisp and delicious you almost don't have to bother with making a dressing. Jim says all you need is a saltshaker.

We grow broccoli and cauliflower and two different kinds of kale. I love kale the way Renata makes it, sautéed with garlic and olive oil and drizzled with lemon. Or baked in the oven so it comes out crisp. We eat it instead of potato chips. Then there are beets that Renata marinates and cauliflower that we use like mashed potatoes. And it's so true about tomatoes—you don't know what a tomato really tastes like until you've eaten a homegrown one. Carrots, peas, string beans. And artichokes—I like how they come back every year. We even grew watercress in the stream until it began to overtake everything, so we replanted it in the garden. *Love* the taste of watercress. We grow watermelon and cantaloupe in the summer. Some years we get a very good crop of corn.

How great to see Michelle Obama plant a vegetable garden at the White House! When you take a patch of earth and grow your own food, you know exactly what you're eating. We placed our garden where it would get the most sun, because vegetables need the energy of the sun, just like humans. We built raised beds for the vegetables out of stone, so we could fill them with really good soil. The eucalyptus trees surrounding the property have very long root systems, and we needed to create a root barrier so they wouldn't infiltrate the garden.

There are trees here and there, to bring in some lovely shade and make the garden look more natural. We planted sycamores and birches and liquid ambers—trees that turn colors in autumn and lose their leaves—because I wanted to experience the change of seasons you get in the east. The fallen leaves get raked up and tossed into the compost heap. Anything we don't eat—eggshells, orange rinds—also ends up there. Some things are fed to the chickens. It's very satisfying, because nothing goes to waste. Everything returns to the earth. P.S. Compost tea is good nourishment for the roses.

This is one afternoon's pickings from the vegetable garden. We'll see what's ready to eat and make a dinner out of it. OPPOSITE, TOP: *I've collected vintage baskets over the years, and keep them out in the garden so they're always handy.* OPPOSITE, BOTTOM: **Fraises des bois,** *perfectly ripe.*

KALE

My Non-Cooking Skills

I can boil water for the corn, but that's about the extent of my culinary gifts. It's not that I'm not interested—I'm fascinated by the chemistry of cooking. I will read a cookbook from cover to cover on a flight and practically taste every dish. I've even taken a few classes. I can give you a meal of Persian rice, moussaka, and chocolate soufflé—but don't ask for anything else. Oh, and hoisin spareribs (easy—just marinate them with honey, molasses, soy sauce, and garlic). But I still can't make coffee.

I really admire people who enjoy cooking and will make these great dinners for family and friends. It's such a loving gesture. I like to plan meals... I just don't like to cook them. Same thing with designing a house. I like all the research and planning, but actually building it is another story. And all that effort to cook somehow destroys the experience of eating for me.

I was in the kitchen the other day, pouring soup Renata had made into cups for Jim and me, and adding a ladle of quinoa and black beans. I thought, Maybe I could do this. But the truth is, I would rather read a book. ❧

PREVIOUS PAGES: *Look at this bounty! How lucky we are.* ABOVE: *Jim asked Nick Fortune, his partner at Oak Country Lumber, to make the vegetable stand for me. I sketched it for him. We put a sink in it so you could wash off the veggies before bringing them into the house, or just eat them right here in the garden.* OPPOSITE: *I love surprises. That's why I wanted these big hedges. What's around the bend? 1,000 roses!*

TO THE BARN

THE BARN
A View Inside

What happens when you walk into a barn? You look up. Suddenly you're in this huge space and your heart expands. You feel like you can breathe. My house is not a traditional barn, and it's not a traditional farmhouse. If it were, you would probably see a staircase in front of you and a narrowish kind of hall with rooms on either side. That's not what I had in mind. I wanted a ceiling that soared. I wanted a room with the scale of a barn and the warmth of wood, but then I wanted to let in the light with large windows so you could see the ocean beyond. How do I design? I don't know. I just visualize it.

OPPOSITE: *As soon as you open the front door, you can see straight through the house to the ocean. Maybe it's because I make films, but to me everything is a shot. Naturally I would have to center the door on the window and frame the ocean.*

The great room is a blend of the rustic and the refined, with weathered posts and beams next to smooth paneling. I designed plate racks to go above the wainscoting, but when I set out the plates they drew attention away from the paintings. I put a desk at the top window up in the loft so I could work facing the view.

The Great Room

It's exhilarating to walk into a space with a 28-foot ceiling, especially when the light is streaming in. Even the ivory plaster takes on a warm sepia tone.

I described my idea for this room to my first architect, who drew something too asymmetrical and modern for me. Then I found another architect or two, who got closer to my vision. I knew it had to be a double-height room with a wraparound balcony, and we went through various versions and came up with this. It's an interesting hybrid, melding elements of Colonial and Arts & Crafts architecture—two periods that have always seemed related to me. (You can trace the similarities in the paneling.)

There's not much furniture as you walk in—just a long library table in the center—because I want your eye to focus on the structure. For authenticity, it was essential to build it with old posts and beams. But I wanted an elegant barn. I always imagined the beams to be rich and polished, like fine furniture. So I had the beams lacquered. My husband thought I was crazy. "How can you touch those old beams?" My answer: "Very easily."

I like the idea of treating a humble material in an elegant way. And I wasn't changing their character—they're still old and adzed (chopped from logs) and cracked. But I wanted to give them more depth. I wanted people to lean against the posts and run their hands over the wood, and you can't do that if it was left in its original state—you'd get splinters! Now they feel like something you'd want to touch.

LEFT, TOP AND BOTTOM: *Sketches allowed me to get a feeling for the space. Do you see those struts on either side of the center post in each rafter? Many people gave me an argument and said they should be straight. I thought it would be more interesting if they were curved.* OPPOSITE: *A two-tiered room deserves a two-tiered chandelier. I didn't have to search far for this one. It was hanging in the foyer when I bought the main house, but it was always too big for that space and looks much better here.*

SOUTHERN INTERIORS

ABOVE, LEFT AND RIGHT: *It's a puzzle. The old floorboards arrive in a pile of random shapes and sizes and then we have to figure out where to put each piece.* BELOW: *The 4 dining chairs against the wall are part of a set of 12. We pull them up to the library table when we're having a dinner party in the great room. The seats are upholstered in a beautiful blue quilted damask to pick up the blue of the screening room next door. I think there should always be a thread connecting one room to another, especially if you can see one from the other.* OPPOSITE: *I began collecting amber glass for this room, because it fits right in with all the sepia tones. When we have dinner in here, we usually set the table with amber glass plates and stemware.*

It's that blend that always fascinates me—the crude and the elegant. The rough-hewn posts and beams also offer a nice contrast to the smooth, more finely crafted wainscoting and balusters, which are in a different finish. They're lighter, the color of honey. I always saw the room in two tones of wood. I'm not sure why. It's just a way of seeing things in subtle tonalities. I think I was very influenced by the old black-and-white movies I saw as a teenager. Because black and white on screen is infinitely subtle—it's really a thousand shades of gray.

Even black is not always black. When I was trying to decide what film stock to use for *Yentl*, I flew to Amsterdam to study the Rembrandts because I felt the film should look like a Rembrandt painting. You don't see the source of light in most of his paintings, and I wanted the light in my movie to feel as if it were coming from within the students, almost as if knowledge was literally enlightening and had given them an inner glow. If I was going to reach for Rembrandt, I needed to see how black the blacks were, and it's interesting—they're not black-black. They're dark brown. There's no hard contrast. The edges of the faces are soft.

You get a similar effect in those old movies. The Rialto theater, next door to my high school, showed foreign films and I used to slip in after class. I saw masterpieces I didn't know were masterpieces, like Akira Kurosawa's *Seven Samurai* and Jules Dassin's *Never on Sunday*. I had no idea they were classics. I just responded to the stories and the filmmaking. The Loew's Kings down the street got the latest Technicolor extravaganzas, like *Guys and Dolls*, and I loved those, too (anything with Marlon Brando!), but there was something about the foreign films in simple black and white that stayed with me. I love all those subtle shifts in tone.

The Library Table

I had the library table made in France and designed the base to echo the curve of the arched braces in the ceiling. There's a stretcher bar at the bottom where you can rest your feet. And I wanted that piece of wood to have more aging on it than the rest of the table, because over the years it would have become worn and scuffed. When you're designing a table, you have to think about all these things. You don't want a table with a lot of legs that will get in the way, and you should be able to expand it for a large party. I had the table made in the same width—48 inches—as two Hepplewhite demilunes from 1800 that I already owned so I could pull the demilunes over to both ends to seat more people. Then I thought, Hmmm, it's a shame to take those tables away from the walls. So I found another two demilunes in the right size, which we store in the basement so we can have them when we need them. ❧

I love the warmth you get from wood, so we used wainscoting—with wallpaper—on the ground floor. But I didn't think it would work up in the loft, where I was planning to hang a large group of paintings salon style. Those walls are done in off-white plaster, a simpler backdrop that doesn't compete with the art.

Here, I was playing with different shades of brown. The floorboards would add another shade and they had to be old. Harold Cole, the man in Connecticut who deals in old wood, found them for me. They're all different. Some of the boards are 21 inches wide, which is very rare. But I didn't have enough wide ones to do the whole room. So I put the wide ones around the edges, where they would show, and hid the narrower ones under the carpet.

Even the so-called experts didn't quite know how to handle these old boards. I swear to God, my guys Vicente and Carlos Ruiz laid them down with nails and glue. It was a big deal, those floors. They had to be hand-sanded as well before you put the stain on. Not too much, because you don't want to destroy the age and the texture, but you don't want to get splinters in your feet, either. It's a fine line between artistry and practicality. Then I turned to Vicente, my resident genius, and said, "I want them to be a honey color. How do we do that?" I even showed him a jar of my favorite honey. He went away and figured it out and came back with exactly what I wanted. Often, a nonprofessional can think outside the box and is willing to try anything. That's why when I direct a movie, I like to use some nonactors for certain roles. They're very natural. Unpredictable.

So now that I have this room, what do we use it for? It doubles as a dining room, because I didn't want to devote a whole other room to dining. That means we needed a hutch to hold dishes and glasses and silverware. I also wanted a pass-through like the one I saw at the Gamble House, which was controlled by ropes. But I couldn't use ropes here because I wanted to be able to open it from either side. That meant we had to figure out how to hide it. You wouldn't know it was there until you press a button underneath the upper cabinet of the hutch and the back panel slides up to connect to the adjacent kitchen. I could give a large dinner party and seat everyone around that library table, although I'm not sure I want all those chairs scraping back and forth on my 200-year-old Aubusson carpet.

We really don't need to eat there or sit there. I'm just happy to walk through it. It's the centerpiece of the house, the great room, the entrance hall. I love to watch people's reactions when I first open the door. They look up, and for a moment, they fall silent. The mouth sort of drops open and then they sigh. That makes me smile.

ABOVE, TOP: *Vicente made some samples for me and managed to get just the right honey-colored shade for the floor.* ABOVE: *For a while, I was torn between plastering or papering the walls and propped up some samples. The wallpaper won. It's hand-printed and looks almost like stenciling. I liked the tone-on-tone effect. Unfortunately, it had to be redone several times. What happens is, you pick something out and since it's all done by special order, they print it for you. But guess what? It doesn't look anything like the sample. So they have to redo it. Not just once, but again and again. Then you get it up on the wall and one piece is darker than the other because it's hand-done. So you have to take that piece off and try to find another piece from the same batch that's closer in color. It's a challenge.*

Most of the doors you're going to see in this house are different on each side. Each room is decorated a bit differently, so each door had to reflect that.

The Door Has Two Faces

The doors in this house became a particular obsession of mine. We used pocket doors to separate the great room from the screening room. The doors are an extension of the wall, so when they're closed and you're looking at them from the great room (left), the panels should be the same height as the wainscoting—65½ inches. But when you come into the screening room (right), the wainscoting is only 42 inches high, so why would you want a 65½-inch panel? Therefore, you need a different design for the door on each side to continue the line. My eye goes to that kind of thing. The panels in the doors have to relate to the walls. If they didn't, it would bother me. ❧

The Screening Room

Imagine the taste of an avocado—a perfectly ripe avocado, not too mushy and not too hard. It has a subtle flavor that's so interesting. Or the scent of a gardenia. You can't capture it. No one has ever been able to make a perfume that smells like the real flower. It's elusive, which is part of why I love it.

I also love subtle colors. The screening room is the color of the sea—a watery blue with a hint of green, and sometimes gray, that can look deeper or paler, depending on the light. Everything here is the same color, basically. I prefer monochromatic rooms. There's no confusion. I don't understand those rooms on the covers of magazines with blue and green and pink and yellow pillows. I don't know where to look. My head gets clogged. When I walk into a room like this that's monochromatic, it puts my mind at rest, my heart at ease. It calms me.

And then something fascinating happens once you sit down. You look around and start to notice things. It turns out that what you first thought was simple is actually quite complex. The blue, in fact, is not all the same. There are subtle differences in tone and texture. One fabric is a chenille, another is a mohair velvet, and then there's a damask (not stiff and pristine—it's washed and that's what makes it look so old and feel so soft). All those slight variations give the room a quiet shimmer. The colors constantly shift and change, like the sea. It's not the same at one in the afternoon as it is at four in the afternoon.

The painting over the mantel is something I bought years ago at a New York art fair from a dealer who had come from Paris. It's by Paul Helleu, a French artist who was known for his portraits during the Belle Epoque period. He was a good friend of John Singer Sargent—another artist whose work I admire. Sargent did a well-known painting of Helleu, sitting next to a boat with his wife, sketching, which now hangs in the Brooklyn Museum. My painting is one of Helleu's rare oil portraits. I bought the painting for this house way before I even began to build it. I just always knew I would do a room in that blue, with brown wood, someday.

The brown wood became my beautiful beams, in that lacquered finish we worked so hard to achieve. I had one contractor who could probably have done this house much faster but he wanted me to leave town, and then he would build the house. But I couldn't leave, because we didn't have everything worked out on paper and there are so many decisions that have to be made day to day (if not hour to hour). But I want to tell you why he thought I was difficult. I walked in one afternoon and his carpenters had put up the two center beams and they were different in size, by

OPPOSITE: *I used to go to the Pacific Design Center every Tuesday to search for fabric, but it was Renata who found the best one. One day I sent her out with my favorite blue sweater to match the color. She went to a remnant store and came back with this beautiful washed damask that's now on the couch. I'll find pieces of new or antique fabric and use them as pillows or throws—the one on the back of the couch is at least 100 years old.*

This was one of the drawings we worked from to build the room. There's actually a door and a window on either side of the fireplace, but I made them all look alike so you can't tell the difference (symmetry, again). At one point, we were thinking of running stone around the base of the whole room, as if it had once held livestock. But I abandoned that idea and went with the wood. Too much stone would take away from the beauty of the fireplace and shorten the height of the room.

maybe an inch and a half, which is a lot to me. Maybe even two inches. He thought that was fine. I said, "Absolutely not." When you walk in, what you first see are those two main beams and you can't have that much difference in size. I thought he should move the thinner one off to the side, where it would be less noticeable. I understand that these are old beams and no two are alike. (By the way, I didn't want them to be alike. Two twenty-three-foot beams could never be exactly the same, unless they were new, which is another thing I didn't want.) But almost two inches off is too much discrepancy for the center of a room. I told him to take them down and find others that were more equal in size. And he got mad. I guess that's why I'm called difficult. That inch and a half matters a lot to me.

Difficult . . . I think it's a very misogynistic attitude, because when a man does this kind of thing, people go, Wow. Isn't that great? He's precise and he really sees and cares about things and he made them change it to get it right But as I said in a speech for Women in Film in 1992, "A man

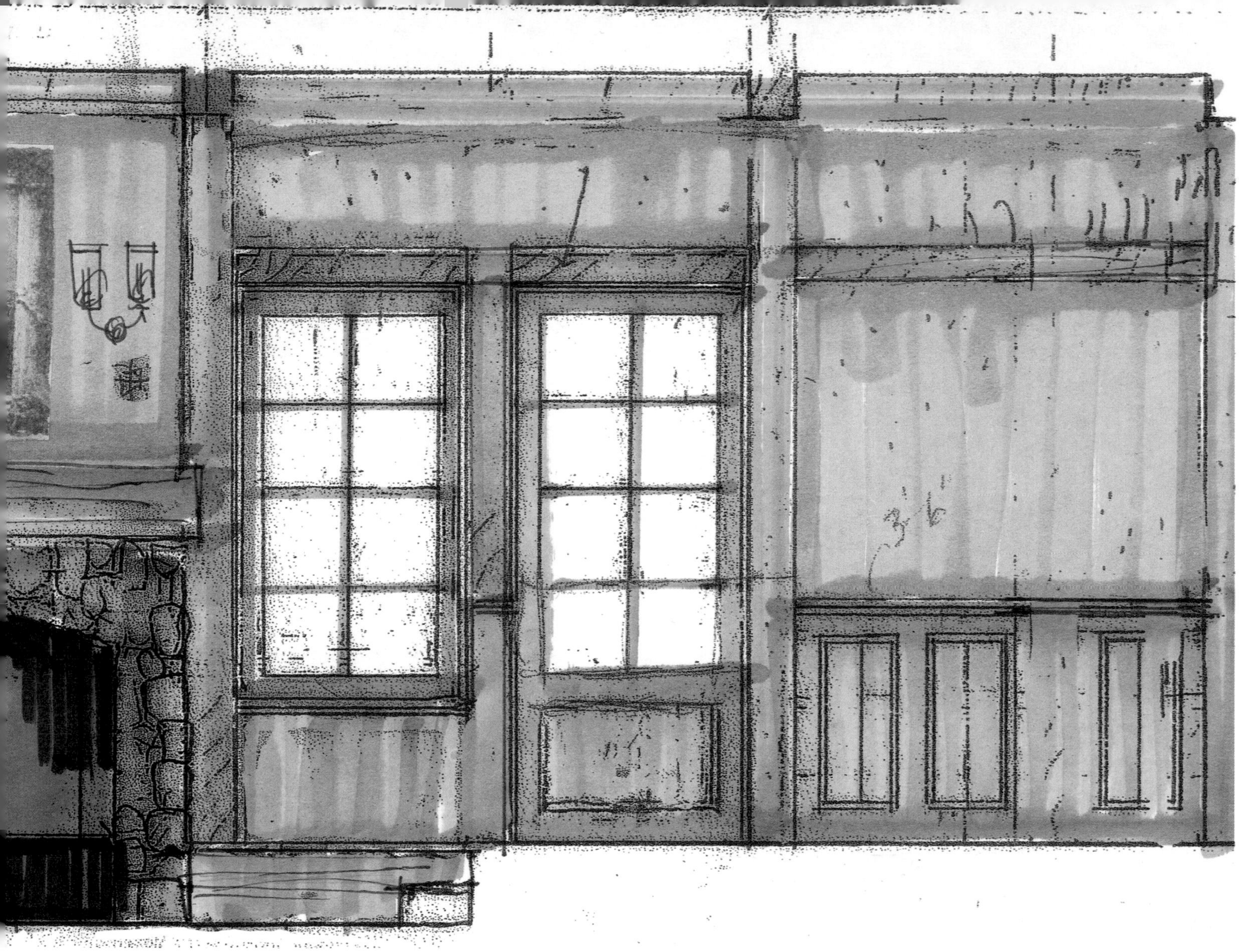

is commanding—a woman is demanding. A man is forceful—a woman is pushy. A man is a perfectionist—a woman's a pain in the ass."

I had never built anything on this scale before—unfortunately, neither had my contractor—and there were plenty of changes along the way. For better acoustics, we were planning to cover the ceiling and the walls above the chair rail with felt. But then I realized this particular color felt comes only in bolts 54 inches wide, which meant that on the bigger sections of the walls and on the ceiling you would have to see seams. So we had to add a piece to the top of the chair rail—another ¾ of an inch—in order to run the fabric horizontally. That way you wouldn't see any seams on the walls. But there was no solution for the ceiling, so we ended up painting it.

I get a headache just talking about it.

And then we had to work out the mechanics of the screening process. John and Charles Massa, who has been my projectionist for almost 40 years, figured out the technology behind this. Now when you want to watch a movie, you press a button and one wall disappears behind the couch to reveal the projector. You don't expect it. Then a screen descends and covers the entire picture window. Press another button and the doors close and all the window shades come down, so you can watch a film at 10 in the morning if you want to. It's heaven.

I used the same damask that's on the couch as an insert in the upholstery on a pair of chairs just opposite the couch. Each insert was finished off with a fringe made of velvety chenille and strips of suede—again, the elegant and the crude. The tufted leather ottoman was designed to have drawers for cocktail napkins and coasters—very practical. My favorite piece of furniture in the room is that Hepplewhite card table, with a hinged top, beside the couch. As soon as I saw the eagle inlay, I had to bid on it at auction. Mansour, a rug gallery, had this rare 1880 Sultanabad with just the right color blue in the background.

You have to be on the site for days, for nights, for weeks in order to know what a house really wants to be. How should the windows look? Here, the ocean is the star, and when you see it through the large center window, you get an unobstructed view. But I added two panes to the side windows in the bay to make a more gradual transition to the multipaned windows by the fireplace.

The Quilts of Gee's Bend
Sargent

When we show a movie, the whole center section of the wall on the right slides down behind the couch so the projectors can project. The set of five folk art portraits on one shelf, depicting a mother and her children, dates back to 1790 and was done by Mr. Boyd of Harrisburg.

A 17-foot-wide screen drops down to cover the whole picture window and the window seat. Just close the shades, dim the lights, and get out the popcorn.

The Silo Staircase

I've always loved barns with silos next to them. Although they mostly held grain, I had always imagined my silo containing a staircase.

I asked the production designer of *Meet the Fockers*, Rusty Smith, to make a scale model of it so we could figure out how many steps we would need to get all the way from the basement to the second floor. And how wide a step would fit inside? I didn't want the staircase to feel cramped. One of my draftsmen found this particular type of spiral staircase on the Internet and I liked it because the balusters were attached to the outside rather than the inside of the steps. Perfect! More width on the step for your foot.

In the midst of all these decisions, I had to leave for a European concert tour. I set up that tour with shopping in mind. The dates were at least four or five days apart, and I went to cities that I hadn't seen or where I wanted to go antiquing. It was so much fun, in between concerts, to go traveling with Jim and another couple. One night in the Loire Valley, we slept in an old mill house (no air conditioning, but great food). Rummaging through their barn, I was surprised and delighted to find the same type of staircase as we had already picked lying on the ground! So it was French in origin. I hadn't known that before. I came across another really tiny, narrow one in a place where we stopped for a Diet Coke. I photographed it and measured the wooden handrail and sent pictures back to my team so they would have samples of different shapes and sizes waiting for my return.

LEFT: *I wanted a mirror opposite the staircase to reflect it and bought one at an auction—a Federal églomisé mirror, crowned with an eagle. It's rare to find an American mirror made this early, around 1800. Most of the mirrors in American rooms during this period came from England. The Sheraton side chairs also date back to 1800 and still have their original paint. They are attributed to John and Thomas Seymour, a father and son who left England to work in Boston and made some of the finest examples of American furniture.* OPPOSITE: *An arched doorway with stone supports leads from the great room to the staircase inside the stone silo. Just beyond the doorway on the right is a closet. I had the transom window lit to display some antique hats.*

Plein Air Painters of California THE NORTH
SOUTHERN INTERIORS

When you look up from the bottom to the top, the staircase takes on the form of a beautiful nautilus shell. It culminates in the eight points of light from the chandelier, which echo the eight rafters on the ceiling.

I was on the Internet for hours every night, e-mailing back and forth about this house, while Jim and I were supposed to be spending alone time together. (It's amazing I'm still married.)

At first I thought the banister should be made of wood, because it would be warmer on your hand. But then all the railings around the loft in the great room were wood, so I decided that this one should be brass. I wanted a runner to go up the steps, but I didn't want to cover all the beautiful old pine or use a complicated rug pattern. So we ended up having a wool runner dyed to match the pine (with different shades of threads so it looked like wood but would be soft under your feet). We wrapped each tread with it, ending just under the bullnose, so you could still see the wood risers.

ABOVE, LEFT: *We drew up many versions of this railing—with wood or brass banisters, with various details on the balusters. (I don't know about you, but I used to get confused about the difference between a banister and a baluster. The banister is what your hand holds on to. The baluster is the vertical post.) In the drawing, plain balusters alternate with brass-knuckled balusters, but we decided to make them all with brass knuckles in the final version* (ABOVE, RIGHT). *At one point, I was going to cover some patches of the stone with white plaster and then wipe it partially off, to duplicate an effect I had seen in an Eric Sloane book on barns. But once the stone was up, I thought, The stonework is so good, I can't cover it up. The grout is recessed, so what you see is stone in all its various shades of gray and brown.*
LEFT: *Those small brass mounts that hold the iron balusters are like bits of jewelry to me.*

The Shakers made utilitarian furniture that also happens to be innately beautiful. Their work is about craftsmanship and consciousness. They understood how to live in this world in a more gentle way.

The Shaker Storage Wall

I love Shaker furniture. It's plain and simple and uniquely American. The way the Shakers often made drawers—in graduated sizes—seems very practical to me. I thought of those drawers when I needed a storage closet at the top of the stairs, for vacuums and all that sort of stuff. I decided to do it in the Shaker style and sketched it out. We made it look like it was part of the wall, just as the Shakers often did. It's built out of pine and stained in two different shades to accentuate the separate compartments. There is something so beautiful about tone on tone. Many pieces of early American furniture—bureaus, especially, and sideboards—were done in two tones of wood. ❧

The staircase is made from welded steel. It had to be attached to a crane and then lifted high above the house and set down into the silo. OPPOSITE: *Will it fit? It was thrilling to see it descend. It took about six hours to set it in place and weld it to the steel frame of the house. Then concrete got poured over the steps, and finally the wood was placed on top of the concrete.*

The Loft/Gym

One day I was watching the movie *Gosford Park* and fell in love with the look of the servants' quarters in the basement of the old English country house where it was filmed. One wall was made of paned glass with dark wood below. I thought, Ah ha! That's how I'll do the walls looking into the gym. I showed the architect the movie, stopped the frame, and said, "That's what I want."

Then I merged that idea with another image I had in my head from the first time I visited the Scripps Institution of Oceanography in San Diego. I was impressed with a scientist's room done in warm wood against creamy white beadboard. It felt very clean and crisp and shipshape. Several years later, antiquing on Cape Cod, I saw that combination again in a shop. Because we live on the sea, a nautical look seemed the right choice for the gym.

For years, I was storing this big universal gym machine that really works every part of your body. The plan was to put it in here. That's why I wanted a television at both ends of the room, so you could watch it no matter which part of the machine you were using. The machine came in a white and black-dotted enamel finish, but I didn't like the black dots so I had it repainted in plain off-white. But then when we finally got it into the room, it turned out that you could see the top of the machine from downstairs, through my *Gosford Park* doors. That wouldn't do. Exercise had to go in favor of aesthetics (not exactly a hard choice). I gave the universal gym to the local fire station.

Then there was the matter of the treadmill. Initially, we planned to have one in front of the big picture window. But the view is so glorious, I said to Jim, "Wouldn't you rather have a double chaise? Then we can sit here and read." That was the end of the treadmill.

We did bring in his stair machine, even though you can see a little piece of that, too, from downstairs, if you look carefully. But that's love. If you love the man, you learn to love his stair machine. It's all about compromise.

Sometimes I wonder, Why did I build this whole house in the first place? All I needed was a screening room and this gym, which I hardly use. I still work out in my makeshift gym in a spare bedroom in the main house. It's closer.

ABOVE: *I've always liked those old schoolhouse light fixtures and hung them in the gym. Just beyond that doorway is Jim's office.* OPPOSITE: *Those are my* Gosford Park *doors up in the loft, leading to the gym. I like those hanging lights in the shape of a bell jar. New, not old, because I couldn't find six antique ones.*

This room feels very New England maritime with the white beadboard and dark rafters. It may be unusual to have a chaise in the middle of a gym, but the view through that window is so beautiful! I wanted to be able to lie there and enjoy it. (So much for exercise!)

ABOVE: *The loft wraps around the top of the great room and allows you to get from one side to the other. When I was trying to figure out the railing, I skimmed through all sorts of molding catalogues in search of just the right baluster, but couldn't find one I really liked.* RIGHT: *Then I found this miniature mahogany staircase (I love miniatures) and liked the way its balusters were carved. Very original. I showed it to the staircase people and asked them to duplicate it. That's why I keep it here, so you can see them together.* BELOW: *I made a mistake with my first desk chair. The back was too high and when you looked up at it from downstairs, it blocked the window. So I had another one made and it was too short.*

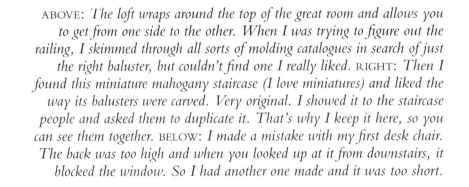

. . . Then I was visiting a friend and saw his antique desk chair (OPPOSITE) *and said, "Oh, that's just the kind of chair I've been looking for." And to my surprise and delight, he insisted I have it. So, in other words, never give up searching for the right thing (and it's great to have generous friends).*

The Federal Lounge

I love the late-afternoon light in the lounge. It picks up all the details of the paneling and brings such warmth to the room.

When I step into an 18th-century room, something about it feels so satisfying to me. I like the pure lines of the woodwork and the graceful fall of the curtains and the simple dignity of the furnishings. Everything is symmetrical. The proportions are pleasing to my eye. I really respond to this period. It's such an interesting blend of elegance and restraint.

I thought it would suit the lounge, which is a small room down the hall from the big screening room. Sometimes you want to be big and sometimes you want to be small, and the lounge is for those intimate moments—a quiet conversation by the fire, a cup of tea on a winter afternoon. And it's equipped with a little area where we can get some water or some ice cream when we're showing a movie. Instead of opening those big sliding doors and disturbing everyone, you can just slip down the hall.

I knew I wanted paneling on the walls, but what color should it be? I thought back to the Federal rooms I'd seen at Winterthur and the American Wing at the Met. There are several Colonial colors I like. Mustard would work, coming off the blue screening room. Maybe I should panel only the fireplace wall.... As I was looking through my books on 18th-century architecture, I noticed that's what they often did. I could still do two glass-fronted cupboards flanking the fireplace and just put wainscoting on the other walls. That might be nice with mustard wallpaper above it.

I pulled a lot of pictures for Jack Taylor, a wonderful art director, who was going to build a model for me. Then one night Jim and I were watching one of those English television shows shot in some great historic house and there was the most beautiful dark blue paneled room. That's it! I immediately redid the whole room in my head. It had to be completely paneled, and it had to be blue ... a different shade from the screening room, but blue ... with mustard accents.

OPPOSITE: *We used real milk paint on the paneling, just as they did in the 18th century. Between coats, you have to put it in the refrigerator or it will spoil. I love that nice chalky finish. It has the softness and the shadows of age. Richard Davis, my painter, is a true artist. The window seat overlooks those stone steps that I spoke of earlier.*
PREVIOUS PAGES: *There's just the right amount of furniture here—two wing chairs, a camelback sofa, tables for your teacups. The portraits on either side of the window are by Erastus Salisbury Field, an American folk artist. On the floor, we used wide pine boards that came out of an old house in Connecticut. They're just waxed, not varnished, which gives you a softer, more authentic period look. P.S. There's a TV in this room, but it's hidden. See if you can find it. No, it's not behind the George Washington portrait.*

It took three sets of carpenters before John found a crew that could actually make the paneling. Even then, when I came back from a short trip, suddenly a panel would be a different shape. "What happened here? This is nothing like the drawing." Some craftsmen don't really relate to paper. They think with their hands. But in this case it was very important to pay attention to every detail.

Detail is the difference between something being ordinary or extraordinary. I wanted delicate Robert Adam details on the mantel and old-fashioned wavy glass on the cabinet doors. I also wanted a particular kind of dentil molding for the cornice line. Most modern dentil molding has a tooth,

ABOVE: *Interior shutters that fold back into the walls are an ingenious Colonial detail. But as the carpenters were building the pockets, I had an idea and asked, "What's going on in the wall behind it?" "Nothing." "Oh. Then let's open it up and build shelves, for books and objects." God forbid we should waste space! The pewter looks perfect here, and of course all the books are in shades of blue.* LEFT: *Here's an example of a mistake! I'm sure someone was trying to please me when he changed the drawing and fancied up the panel by the window seat. But it didn't look right. The lines of the raised panel should just die into the side of the window seat, as you see in the finished version* (OPPOSITE). *The Hepplewhite mirror used to hang in my New York apartment. Asian pears and Butterscotch roses are the perfect color for this room.*

I looked through all kinds of books for inspiration and thought back to all the historic houses and museums I've visited and used a detail here, a detail there . . . everywhere a detail.

and then a shallower tooth, a tooth and a shallower tooth, and so on. But I wanted a tooth and then empty space, like I have on an 18th-century cabinet I own. What's important is that space. Why? Because it creates shadows. I searched through dozens of catalogues . . . became a student of all the various types of moldings. But I couldn't find what I wanted and ultimately had to have them custom made by El & El Wood Products. Thank god the head of the company, Cathy Vidas, was a fan of mine.

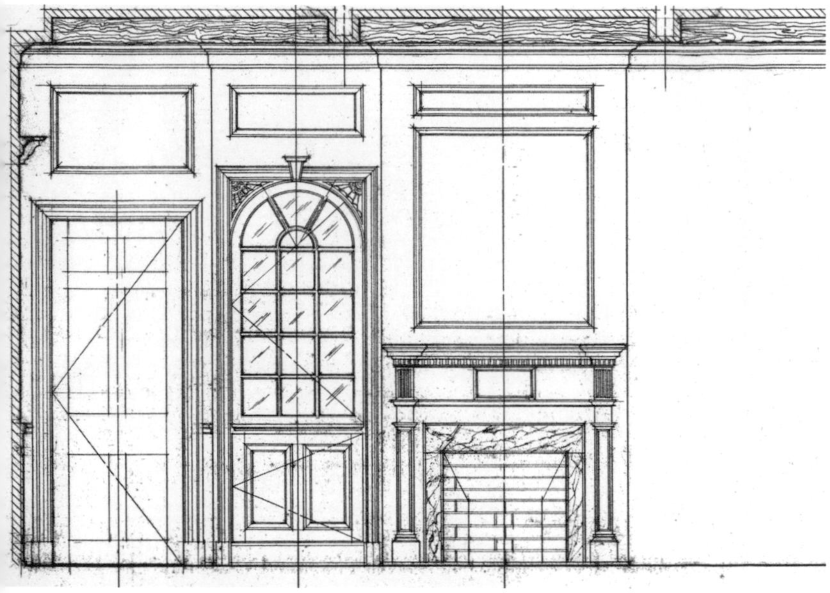

But here's the irony. This is one of the few rooms where we were working from actual plans, with specific dimensions, and yet the cabinets are three inches narrower than in the drawings. Three inches. That's a lot. If there's a discrepancy like that, why didn't the carpenter ask the contractor and why didn't the contractor ask the art director and why, above all, didn't somebody ask me? It's fascinating how something like that happens. Apparently, the problem is measuring. It's one way in the drawings and another way in reality. I still can't figure that out, but I have to let it go. What I wonder is, Did this sort of thing also happen back in the 18th century?

TOP: *I saw this picture in a book and liked the rounded cabinets within rectangular paneling and did my own version with glass doors.*
MIDDLE: *I had the panel over the fireplace made to fit my painting of George Washington. You can see George in the model* (BOTTOM). *One contractor wanted to use MDF—medium-density fiberboard—for the paneling to save money and, he said proudly, it won't crack. I said no. The point is, you want to use what they used in the 18th century and you want it to crack. I don't mind cracks. They're the marks of age. It's like that Leonard Cohen lyric: "Ring the bells that still can ring. Forget your perfect offering. There is a crack, a crack in everything. That's how the light gets in."*

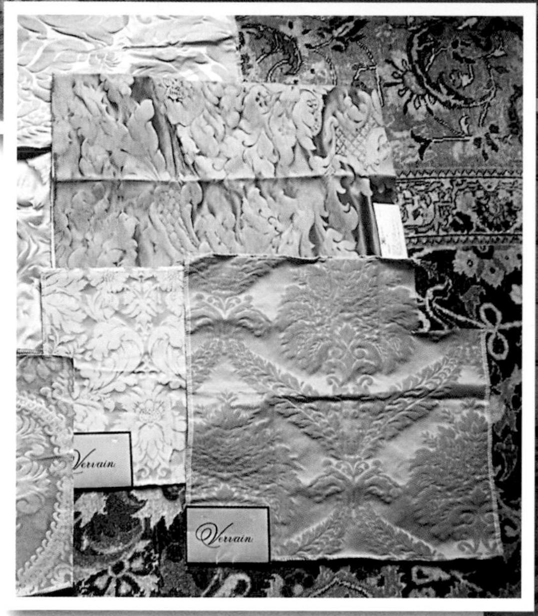

Sometimes I'm Impatient . . .

Too impatient to wait until I find the exact right thing. So I'll just get something in the meantime because my need for instant gratification is strong. Perhaps that's because my father died so young. I like to get things done fast. And I hate waste. Instead of looking for new furniture, I tried to speed up the process by having the old George Smith furniture from my New York apartment recovered in red silk velvet (to match a red and mustard rug I was considering). It looked all right in the drawing, but when I put it in the room, all of a sudden the red became too much. So I had the room sketched up with mustard yellow upholstery instead. Better, but something was still off. Then I realized the problem was the furniture itself. Nothing is as comfortable as a George Smith sofa, but it had the wrong silhouette. When a space is so architecturally pure, with all those 18th-century lines, you cannot furnish it with an overstuffed sofa. Think of the period, with women in big round skirts. Once you sat down, you could never get up! I don't want the set to be inaccurate, even though no one's filming it. The George Smith furniture had to go. Before I chose the final upholstery fabrics, I laid them against the blue and mustard Persian rug I finally bought to see which had the proper tone. ❧

The Mackintosh Hall

Certain architects excite and inspire me.
It wasn't enough just to look at pictures in books.
I wanted to be in those rooms.

When I was designing this house, I thought back to all the architects I loved and wanted to represent here. I wasn't worried about the changes in style. I thought it would work. And there was no need to justify it, but if someone asked, I had my script in my head. Perhaps the family who bought the property liked Federal architecture and built that part of the house first. Or maybe the lounge and the blue bathroom are all that remain of an even earlier house. Then sometime after 1904, they decided to expand. They might have stopped in Glasgow on a tour of Europe and been inspired by Charles Rennie Mackintosh's work. Or they might have visited a friend in Pasadena and walked through one of the houses recently built by Charles and Henry Greene. They could have subscribed to *The Craftsman* and become familiar with Gustav Stickley.

Mackintosh, Greene & Greene, and Stickley were great architects, and I am enthralled by their work. Even though they lived in different parts of the world—Scotland, California, and New York—they shared a common vision: a concept of architecture as a complete art. They didn't just design the exterior of a building and stop there. If you were an architect, wouldn't you want to design the interior, too? They took their ideas down to the smallest detail. They created complete environments. And they were all part of the Arts & Crafts movement, which valued the singular object over the output of a machine. They advocated a return to craft and individuality. When you touch a chair or a table that any of these men made, you're touching wood that has passed through someone's hands. It has been treated with respect.

This vestibule is my homage to Mackintosh. It was built around a Mackintosh cabinet that I've owned for many years. Original pieces of his furniture are hard to find, because so many were destroyed. His reputation didn't really take off until after he had died. Because oak is a wood

OPPOSITE: *This door is made of honey-colored pine, because we're coming off the honey-colored pine paneling in the great room. But on the other side, in the Mackintosh hall, the wood changes to oak. And the hardware changes as well. The handles* (ABOVE) *are no longer brass, but bronze . . . that dark, almost blackened bronze. And in the Greene & Greene library just beyond, the oak changes to mahogany. The different woods lead you from one style to another.*

ABOVE, LEFT: *The Vienna Secession-style bookcase is a nod to artists like Josef Hoffmann and Gustav Klimt, who admired Mackintosh and invited him to design a room for the Vienna Secession exhibition in 1900.* ABOVE, RIGHT: *The rose in the hammered copper tile reminded me of Mackintosh. For him, the rose represented art. It was "the symbol of all that is noble—and beautiful—and inspiring," as he wrote.* OPPOSITE: *The metalwork on the Mackintosh cabinet is very fine and thin, which gives this large piece a certain delicacy. The amazing drawings (just prints, wish I had the originals!) are by Margaret MacDonald, Mackintosh's wife and collaborator. In 1927, the year before he died, he wrote in a letter to her, "You must remember that in all my architectural efforts you have been half if not three-quarters of them." I love that he acknowledged her contribution to his work.*

he often used, I chose it for the wainscoting. I found the copper tiles one night on the Internet and liked the fact that they were embossed with a rose. It's a motif that reappears through all his work. I had them inset into the paneling. I hope he would have approved.

I used to own a beautiful Mackintosh light fixture, but I sold it at auction. Who knew I was going to do this room? I tried for the longest time to make another Mackintosh-type fixture, but the mock-up just didn't look right to me . . . too big, too weird, too wrong. But then I remembered that up in the attic I had two reproduction Mackintosh sconces I had found in an antiques shop and bought, just in case. I asked Vicente if he could combine them, and he cut off the backs and bolted them together. I'm a realist. If I can't find an original piece or if one doesn't exist, I'll use a reproduction.

Of course I still can't get that original fixture out of my head. It's another one of those things I never should have sold.

The Greene & Greene Library

When I first walked into the Gamble House in Pasadena, designed by Charles and Henry Greene in 1908, I was overwhelmed by its beauty and astonished by its detail. I had never seen wood that looked so soft, so touchable. Every piece was rounded. There were no sharp edges. I wanted to run my hand along the woodwork, not just the stair rail. The mortise-and-tenon joints were finished with ebony pegs. And the beams, gently curved at the ends and strapped together with iron, looked like something out of a Japanese temple.

That was in the 1980s. When I went back years later, I really paid attention to the floor—there was something so intriguing about the pattern. But I couldn't quite make it out because the rug was covering it. I asked the curator if we could please, just for a moment, pick it up so I could see what was going on underneath. It turned out the floor was laid in an elongated chevron pattern . . . slim eight-foot-long boards, two and one-quarter inches wide, radiating to all four sides from a point in the middle. Can you imagine the mathematical genius of that? A point in the center where everything converged, and then each of the chevrons on all four sides began with these triangles that were also centered on the fireplace or a window or a door. I *love* things like that. You don't even see it because it's under the rug, but you know it's there. Then there was the stained glass in the doors. And those exquisite light fixtures, oh my god! The whole house was a work of art. How did they ever achieve such an extraordinary level of craftsmanship? Apparently Frank Lloyd Wright, another of my favorite architects and no slouch himself when it came to detail, wondered as well. He once told the brothers, "I don't know how you do it."

When I see something as beautiful as this, I can't stop thinking about it.

I wanted to see more and bought every book I could find on the Greenes' work. There's something interesting in the fact that their very first client was a woman and that women were responsible for most of their commissions. These were well-educated, politically and socially progressive women who often knew one another and recommended the Greenes to other friends. They responded to the natural beauty of the work. It's clear from the records that Mary Gamble was more closely involved in designing the Gamble House than her husband, David (who apparently did have an opinion, but only about the den).

LEFT: *We put various elements together . . . the octagonal hanging lights from the Pratt House, the railings from the Gamble House sleeping porch, the frieze from the Thorsen House . . . to create our own version of Greene & Greene.* PREVIOUS PAGES: *When we were designing furniture for this room, I added the bolster pillows to the sofa and trimmed them with Chinese knots and tassels, to relate to the Chinese influences in the work. How many times have you bumped into a coffee table? Rounded corners are more humane. The unusual muntins on the cabinet doors are a replica of those in the Thorsen House. I love old leather-bound books. For this room they had to be in certain colors—burgundy, brown, or mustard.*

The majestic curve of the beams is taken from the Gamble House living room, but then I added the tapered king posts in the center, like those in the attic of the same house.

Look at the floor. The boards are laid in a long chevron pattern that radiates from the center and finishes in a small triangle at the midpoint of each wall. The carpet is an antique Agra in shades of burgundy and smoky mustard, and we picked up that mustard in the paint on the walls.

ALBUM

I had this two-story space and wanted to build a library, so I thought to myself, What would Greene & Greene do? I described what I had in mind to Robert Shachtman, an architect who happens to do very artistic drawings, and he drew it up for me. But who could make it? Would it even be possible to do anything like that today?

Turns out that someone had, at a hotel in La Jolla, The Lodge at Torrey Pines, where Jim and I had stayed. It's built in the style of Greene & Greene, and the people there were kind enough to give me the name of the man who did a lot of the custom woodwork. Brian Krueger is a master craftsman and very into detail, like me, so we really got along. We began putting it all together.

My library is not a replica of any one particular Greene & Greene room, but sort of an improvisation on their melodies. I did a riff on the Gamble House doors and added built-in seats between the bookshelves. I liked many details from the Thorsen House in Berkeley, including the painted frieze around the living room ceiling, with flowers trail-

ABOVE, LEFT: *The reproduction Greene & Greene rocker stands next to a Tiffany floor lamp with all its original attachments for books and flowers.* ABOVE, RIGHT: *You can pull out a book, sit right here under the light, and read a bit to decide if you want to continue.* LEFT: *The Greenes usually did natural linen curtains or shades, and then I added my own spin with a top layer of lace.*

ing from its *U*-shaped corbels. In our version, it's not exactly the same flower, and I changed the colors from an orangey pink to a burgundy rose. The beams were inspired by those in the Gamble House, which are made of Douglas fir, because that's what the Greenes often used. It was a local wood for them. I remember when someone tried to persuade me to use Douglas fir beams in the great room, because it would have been easier than importing eastern white pine from across the country. But Douglas fir is a western wood. They wouldn't have used it on the East Coast. And I wanted an eastern feeling in that part of the barn, so I just couldn't do it.

Brian made the furniture specifically for this room, because it's extremely rare to find original pieces. (Thank god. They should stay where they belong, in the original houses! And in museums.) When I was at a textiles show in Massachusetts, I saw some red wool drapes with distinctive leather embroidery that looked very Arts & Crafts. So I bought the drapes, cut out the embroidery, and had it stitched onto some deep, rich velvet that I used for the pillows and the upholstery. I love this velvet. It's the color of a good Merlot.

I wanted a similar color for the tiles on the fireplace, and it took a few attempts to get just the right shade in a matte finish. Then we tried to replicate the inlaid flowers that I had liked on the master

Behind the Ebony Pegs

By the way, it's a myth that the Greenes never used nails. They used not only nails but also screws as part of the construction process. They just never left them exposed. Nails were basic to the framing of the house. If a screw was needed to support a joint, the head was recessed below the surface of the wood, and the hole was filled in with little ebony pegs. All that amazing joinery—the way one piece of wood is nestled into another—is not just pretty. It's functional. And it was beautifully executed by Peter and John Hall, two immensely gifted Swedish brothers who served, respectively, as contractor and mill-shop supervisor.

There is nothing in a Greene & Greene house—wood, metalwork, art glass, tile, brick—that hasn't been touched by the human hand. That's what is so exceptional about their work. At its peak it was glorious, but then the partnership dissolved, although the brothers remained close. Did the intensity of all that ravishing detail become too much? There were rumors of a breakdown. Henry tried to carry on the practice; Charles retreated to Carmel. After Mrs. Blacker died, the furniture custom made for the house was put out on the lawn and sold! Can you imagine that? It's so sad. It wasn't until 1952 that the brothers were finally recognized by the American Institute of Architects and given an award, just a few years before they died. ❧

bedroom fireplace in the Blacker House, also in Pasadena. A very good tile man made some tile flowers, but they were never quite right. The colors were too bright. I said, "It's too much contrast for me." The flowers needed to be darker, more subtle. And then the guy gave up. He said, "I can't do it." And I completely understood. I was tired after three and a half years—that's how long it took to do this suite of rooms—and I said, "Let's just use the plain tiles." It kind of killed me to give up on it.

Instead, I decided to do an inlay on the cabinet doors above the fireplace. Brian had tiny birds carved out of wood and added mother-of-pearl clouds and water.

There comes a point when you have to compromise, and sometimes the compromise leads to something better. I go through this when I'm directing a film as well. I remember one day on *The Prince of Tides* when I was trying to get a shot that Pat Conroy, the brilliant author of the novel on which the film was based, described in the book, of the sun and the moon in the sky at the same time. But neither would cooperate—they were hiding behind clouds. So I thought, Okay, What else can I get? I had the mother and children sitting on the dock. At least give me a sunset. And thank god, at the last moment the sun appeared and as it set over the treetops it colored the scene with this beautiful pink light. That's the challenge of compromise. You have to go with what the universe presents. And one hopes that's enough.

The Green Greenes

Now that I was completely seduced by Greene & Greene, I *really* wanted to see the inside of the Blacker House. But because it's not on a tour where you can pay to get in, I had to track down the owner. He agreed to show me around, but only if I let him borrow a pair of Greene & Greene sconces I owned so he could copy them for the house.

On the day of my visit it was 104 degrees outside, but inside the house it was cool as a cucumber. How did they do that without air conditioning? That's the brilliance of the Greenes' design. They built in a lot of cross-ventilation, starting in the basement and going all the way up to the attic, where there were places for hot air to escape. Interior windows kept the air moving, and inside every closet door was a fan. Deep overhanging eaves also sheltered the rooms from the sun. Think how much energy we could save if we followed their example!

Here's another fascinating detail. When we were in the upstairs foyer, the owner brought over a chair and told me to stand on it and touch the ceiling. I was surprised—it was made of canvas. Why? I later asked architects and HVAC people, but just got blank stares. The answer died with the Greenes, but maybe it provided another layer of air—and therefore insulation—between the ceiling and the attic. They often used canvas on walls as well. Plaster cracks; canvas doesn't. So smart. ❧

PREVIOUS PAGES: *The lightly hammered copper surrounding the fireplace was treated with acid to get just the right mellow tone . . . more matte, like the Dirk Van Erp fire tools on the left. Then the mother-of-pearl inlay on the cabinet above was too white and too bright, so I asked Brian to stain it. The stained-glass door leads to the napping room.*

The objects in the cabinet represent another branch of the same movement that inspired Greene & Greene. While the brothers were building homes in Pasadena, Archibald Knox was designing Art Nouveau objects, like these clocks, for Liberty & Co. in London. The silver and enamel frames are also from Liberty & Co. and date back to the turn of the last century. For the period look, I wanted wooden shelves, but we made them with glass in the middle so the light can shine through.

The Napping Room

This room is in the octagonal silo on the back of the house. Initially, I was thinking of building a recording studio where the library is now, and this was going to be my vocal booth. Then the technicians came and said, Well, this won't work because sound has to bounce off the walls this way and that way and you really should have a multilayered cement floor . . .

I said, Forget it. It was way too technical for me and a pain in the neck. I decided I'd rather take a nap.

In my napping room. What else could you build in a space this small? It's like being in a boat. Jim and I both love boats . . . the way everything is neatly fitted and tucked away. Here a little step pulls out and you climb up to the bed, because I wanted the mattress to be right beneath the windowsill, so you can look out and see the ocean. And isn't there something wonderful about climbing up into a bed? It reminds me of going to England for the first time and sleeping in those big, high featherbeds. It just feels cozier.

You can settle into the pillows and read a bit before you fall asleep (from the book, sometimes). It's a quiet, private spot . . . a little retreat where I can go to escape . . . or have a rendezvous with my husband.

A stained-glass door, inspired by the front door of the Gamble House, leads from the library to the napping room, and from there you go through another stained-glass door to the bathroom. I wanted something more delicate than the oak tree on the Gamble House door and did my own version of a flowering tree, with a thinner trunk. The Greenes had their tree positioned in the middle, but I thought mine should be a narrower tree on the far side of each door so I would have room for flowers at the ends of the branches. And when you're lying in bed, the branches will seem to be reaching toward one another.

To make the doors, I went to Judson Studios and worked with David Judson, the great-grandson of the man who had made stained glass for the Greenes. He showed me samples of all the colors, and it was hard to find the right shade of burgundy for the flowers. The rest of the tree is in different shades of brown and green. Then I had to pick a color for the leading, which can be anything from black to gold to copper. I wanted something very muted and chose a dark browny-grayish-black that looked old, not new. It took a long time to make those doors, but they did a fabulous job.

LEFT: *I climbed up on the bed to get this shot, which shows how the branches on the two doors stretch toward each other. (By the way, the room's not tilted; it's just the wide-angle lens.)* OPPOSITE: *If we need an extra bed for a guest, she could sleep here. The mattress had to be custom made to fit this odd shape. The Old California Lantern Co. did a great job on the light fixtures. The hexagonal shape of this one, modeled after an original in the Culbertson House in Pasadena, echoes the angled wall and casts a lovely shadow. The blinds in here had to be electric, so you can click a button and change them without crawling over the bed.*

The Greene & Greene Bathroom

I don't think Greene & Greene ever used wallpaper but I thought it would be interesting here. I liked the fact that it had these two greens—an olive and a bluer green, like the green matte glaze on Teco pottery. It's incongruous to see those two colors together, but I love that rub. I love it in music, too—the atonality of two notes right next to each other. There's something a little off about it that I respond to.

I was inspired by the sideboard in the Thorsen House dining room and thought it would make a beautiful vanity. We fitted our version with a burgundy sink I had found years ago (along with a burgundy tub and toilet) and saved for this house. Then I wanted burgundy porcelain on the handles of the faucet and had to have white porcelain specially painted and glazed. The burgundy tiles were also custom made. The proportions of the vanity and the mirror were all worked out to leave enough space for that thin strip of burgundy on the backsplash. ❧

ABOVE, LEFT: *Of course, the towels had to be burgundy.* ABOVE, RIGHT: *I had tiles made in the same blueish green as the wallpaper and used them around the tub.* OPPOSITE: *The same tiles, in a shiny finish, create a pattern in the shower stall. The light fixture is modeled on one from the Duncan-Irwin House, also in Pasadena, but I modified the size for this small room and changed the shape and type of glass. Mine is made out of iridescent glass to match the sconces.*

The Stickley Office

In this room you can once again see my love for a monochromatic palette. It's simpler. And then if you really study it, you can pick out all the nuances.

We've gone from Colonial honey-colored pine to Mackintosh's medium-brown oak to Greene & Greene's deep, rich mahogany, and now to an even darker oak with Gustav Stickley. I tried to soften the transition between the work of these great architects by having the wood gradually get darker and darker as we move from room to room. For me, the change in color reinforces the change in styles. And nothing is jarring, even though every floor, every door casing, every piece of hardware is different. The wood carries you through, so it all seems to flow naturally.

I've had this Stickley furniture for years, first in my office in my New York apartment and now here. But I wouldn't want to sit on that couch if it was still upholstered in the brown leather it came in, which looked too hard, too dark, too heavy to me. I know that's the way Stickley sold it, but I had it recovered in dusty rose velvet.

I'm only a purist when it suits me.

Putting this rose velvet on this wood furniture just *feels* right. And then I wanted a lighter dusty pink on the walls. It's unusual to have a pink office, but I seem to love that color. Years ago, I saw a period room at the Metropolitan Museum of Art in a similar pink, and I've never forgotten it. It's those images embedded in my brain again.

I'm attracted to the combination of the masculine and the feminine, like the masculine solidity of the wood counterbalanced with the feminine softness of the velvet. It's that same combination I'm always drawn to . . . the rough and the smooth, the crude and the elegant, the earthy and the spiritual. There is something compelling about the tension of opposites. It's not either/or. It's both.

LEFT: *Arts & Crafts artists shared a common bond and influenced one another. The pattern on the Stickley pillow is reminiscent of Margaret MacDonald's work.* OPPOSITE: *I collected different kinds of art pottery—Rookwood, Roseville, Van Briggle—in similar shades of pink. Many years ago, Heath made that set of dishes for me with that beautiful matte glaze in that luscious color.* PREVIOUS PAGES: *The furniture is all Stickley, except for that long bench in front of the couch and the two end tables, which I had made. I put rose-colored tiles on top of the tables and added a hidden drawer. Not sure Stickley would have approved, but it's practical. The photographs are by Edward S. Curtis.*

The secret to the pink on the walls was a first coat of rust-colored paint, and then over that a pink with a little gray in it. But when we went back to do another coat, we could never duplicate the color. So I left it alone. The chairs are upholstered in pale pink suede. The desk lamp is by Dirk Van Erp.

The Master Suite

The first bed I ever bought was a four-poster—tall, dark, and Jacobean, carved out of oak. I found it in one of those antiques shops on University Place in New York, and it looked great to me, coming from a cold-water flat where the whole bedroom was only half as big as that bed.

I've always loved the warmth of a four-poster. Back when there was no such thing as central heating, you just lit the fire and climbed in and closed the bed curtains. It's cozy inside. And there's something very comforting about a canopy. It's protection from the sky falling down on you. (Although the canopy could fall on you, too!)

We only have one bedroom in the barn. And of course it's furnished with a mahogany four-poster bed, modeled after one I saw years ago in a magazine. I liked its elegant lines and height, so I found out where it was made (London) and ordered one for my bedroom in New York. The reason I had to have it custom built is because you can't find an antique bed that's bigger than a double, and when you have a partner in life, you need more room. But not too much room. I always think king-size beds are too big and queen-size beds are too small. So I make them in between—66 inches wide (in between the 60-inch queen and the 72-inch king) and 82 inches long (in between 80 and 84). Those proportions feel exactly right to me. It's the perfect size for people who love each other. You're close when you want to be close, but you have enough room to turn over and not bump into each other or get a foot in your mouth—no, wait, that foot belongs to Samantha, who also sleeps with us. Sammie is smart. She doesn't want to get kicked, so she sleeps above our heads.

Months after I ordered the bed, on the way home from Greece (my dear friend Steve Ross had invited us to join him on a sailing trip through the islands), I stopped off in London to see how the work on it was coming along. As soon as I saw it, I thought, Oh my god, How am I going to get this into my bedroom on the 22nd floor of a New York apartment building? There was no way it was going to fit into the elevator. "Guess what, guys. You're going to have to miter the corners of the canopy so it comes apart." This was turning out to be a very expensive visit. But the changes were completely necessary. It wouldn't have worked otherwise. And then the bed hangings, with all those beautiful, precise pleats inside the canopy and around the edges, made up of two fabrics—a blue and white Ralph Lauren stripe and a natural vanilla English cotton—cost double what the bed itself cost. I remember thinking, This is ridiculous. But now I'm glad I did it. The workmanship is impeccable. Here it is, 20 years later—the bed has been moved across an ocean and a continent—and every single pleat still looks perfect.

OPPOSITE: *I had this portrait of a woman by F. W. Simmons in my New York bedroom and now she hangs here. The mahogany cabinet at the foot of the bed holds a TV. It seemed so simple, but it wasn't. At first I hired someone who built it way too wide and way too deep for a flat-screen TV. But then you don't want it too narrow, either, because it would look phony. I wanted it to look like a real piece of furniture.*

I loved the hand-carved details on this four-poster bed and the rosette in the middle of the canopy. The headboard is simple, high enough to actually rest your head, and well padded—very important—with reading lights so you can read comfortably in bed (placed low enough so you can turn them off as you're falling asleep). Vicente made a little set of steps, which you can't see but they're on the right side, so Sammie can go up and down.
A pair of 18th-century Chippendale mirrors flanks the bed. The chest on the right is actually a desk, which I spruced up with more elegant hardware. A desk makes a great nightstand.

I reused many elements from my New York bedroom in this room. The blue and white striped wallpaper is the same. It matches the fabric I used for the canopy, and had made into drapes in New York. When I sold that apartment, I took the drapes down off the wall so if I ever needed the fabric, I'd have it. Lucky I did, because now it's discontinued. That's why I save a lot of things. You never know....

OPPOSITE: *When I saw this old corner cabinet in a shop in Pasadena, I had to buy it. It was just the height and happened to have practically the same moldings as my corner fireplace. It solved the problem of what to put on the other side of the window. My husband (who still thinks I'm wrong) wanted a door to the terrace, but I couldn't live with that asymmetry.* ABOVE: *Everything in the cabinet is in the same colors as the room. I found that pair of turn-of-the-century shoes in Paris. The leather is delicately beaded, which is something you don't see nowadays. The little half shades for sconces are in the same pink as the lusterware.* LEFT: *I bought the doll, called a* marotte, *in Paris as well. She has a German bisque head and twirls around on a stick, like something a jester might carry . . . and plays music to boot.*

I bought that painting of the woman in the pink dress over twenty years ago. I like her because she looks thoughtful, and she's wearing a black velvet neckband, the kind I often wear myself. It's so period, and yet so contemporary. I always put pink flowers in the room, to match her dress. The colors here are all the softest blues and off-whites, with touches of pink. When I visited the White House (where, by the way, the Queen's Bedroom has pink walls and a Sheraton four-poster), I noticed the mahogany doors had white casings around them. They were just so beautiful, and I did the same thing here—but only on the bedroom side. On the dressing room side, the doors have mahogany casings. Every detail is different in every room. That's what took me so long.

ABOVE, LEFT: *The antique armoire is delicately carved and mirrored—and practical.* ABOVE, RIGHT: *I first saw those tiles surrounding the fireplace in a book of period details, and was going to try to have them copied from the picture. Then I walked into Waterworks and, to my delight, somebody had thought of it before me. There was the same tile, only it was white on white. I wanted it in the colors of the room, with a blue ribbon and flowers in slightly different shades of pink* (BELOW)*. It took a long time to get the colors exactly right. You have to have patience, as it says in the Talmud. But it's hard for me. Patience is not one of my virtues.*

On the chairs and ottoman, I did a little kick pleat at the corners, with an off-white rounded insert against the pale blue. It falls gracefully on the floor, like a ball gown. Do you see that little window up top? I thought it would be nice to lie in bed and see the moon, so we built an eyebrow window. I call it my moon window. And then we had to figure out a way to block the light when we slept. Now we can push a button and shades go down over the picture window and a little half-moon shade goes up over the moon window—outside. That's one for modernity.

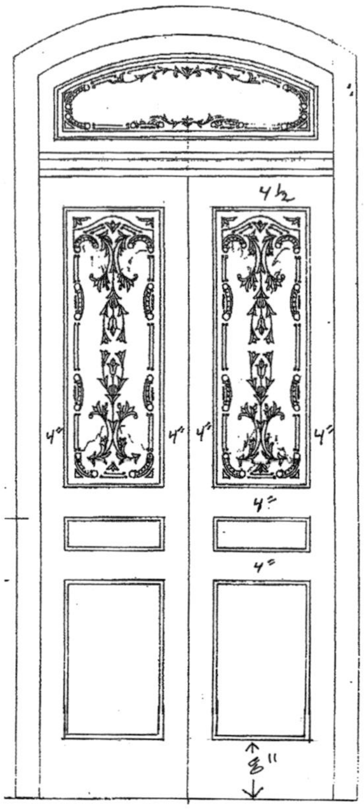

The door between the bedroom and the dressing room is solid mahogany, but between the dressing room and the tub room, I added etched glass. It's a lovely detail I've seen in Victorian houses, and the etched glass also lets more natural light into my little room, so it's practical as well.

LEFT: *I found a good etched-glass maker, Andreas Lehmann, in* Traditional Building *magazine and he worked from this sketch.* BELOW, LEFT: *My makeup table is bathed in natural light—essential if you're going to look natural.* BELOW, RIGHT: *The two brass panels on top slide apart. It's a detail I designed to hide my makeup.* OPPOSITE: *This view, looking from the tub room through the dressing room to the bedroom, shows the finished doors. I hung pictures of women in period dress . . . wearing only shades of white, pink, and powdery blue.*

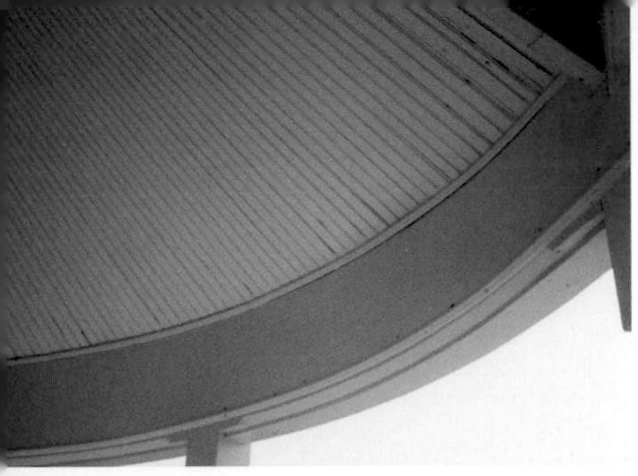

TOP: *The original Stanford White ceiling that inspired my version.* MIDDLE: *A chandelier in the bathroom? Why not? I've always had one, since my first grown-up apartment on Central Park West. It adds romance and light.* BOTTOM: *The planks on the floor are laid to echo the pattern on the ceiling.*

The tub room is at the top of the rear silo, so it's got that wonderful octagonal shape. I tried something very ambitious on the ceiling. Around 1987, I went to Montauk with Peter Larkin, a production designer, to see the Stanford White houses. I was thinking about building a house, and we were doing research. I love the research period, by the way. That's the most fun for me. You're not in the construction and aggravation mode, you're in the inspiration and learning mode. I could do research for years.

It's funny, but certain houses just get imprinted on my brain in such a powerful way. White was commissioned to do this group of homes, known as the Seven Sisters, for a group of friends back in 1879, and one of them had the most amazing ceiling on a rounded porch made of vertical beadboard. On the flat side nearest the house, each board was about an inch and a half wide, and then it ran 10 or 12 feet up to a point. And at that point the beadboard was so thin it looked like the head of a pin. How in the world was that done?

Years later, I was talking to Ingrid Sischy, the former editor of *Interview* magazine, and describing this ceiling to her and she said, "That's my house!" She told me that no one had ever been able to duplicate that ceiling. It was made by barrel makers back in 1880 and no one has figured out the technique they used. My carpenters couldn't do it. So I changed the design to go horizontally rather than vertically, and that was difficult enough. Nobody could figure that out, either, for the longest time. I actually had three different sets of carpenters try it. Third time lucky. It was so hard to line up the beadboard so that each board met, precisely, on either side of each rafter. When the framers put the silo up, the walls weren't perfect. Then the plasterers came, and the plaster wasn't perfect. If you didn't line up each section of the wall exactly, the whole thing went out of whack. It was a constant battle, adding plaster to this or that wall, trying to straighten it out. That's the hardship—and the fun—of getting it right.

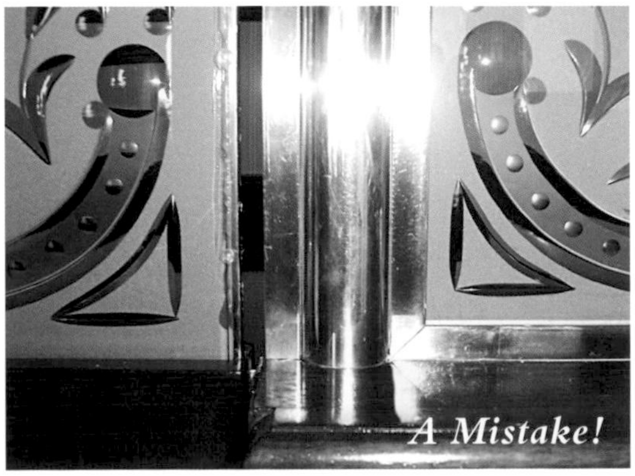

A Mistake!

Recently, I was having dinner with my friend Ron Meyer. His house was designed by the architect Charles Gwathmey. I was talking about how wonderful it must be to work with a fantastic architect who really knows what he's doing. He must have had it all

When they installed this glass enclosure, the etching on the two panels didn't line up (OPPOSITE). *One started about half an inch higher than the other. It had to be redone, of course.*

down on paper. And Ron said, "Well, that's not necessarily true. Certain things had to be redone four or five times. Charlie would come in and look at a wall and say, 'No, it really should go like this.'"

I actually felt better. So it happens with all those big guys, too. In other words, there is the idea and then there is the reality, and it doesn't always come across in a drawing. A drawing is a drawing. It's a flat, nondimensional thing. Even a model, when you actually start to build, is not always accurate, especially if somebody measured wrong. Ron remembered Charlie saying to the workmen, "If you build this one-sixteenth of an inch off, it won't work." And that's the truth. To build something right requires that kind of precision. By the way, I went to Cirque du Soleil the other afternoon and saw this amazing juggler. It reminded me of the first newspaper article I ever wrote. I was 22, and starring in *Funny Girl* at the time. I started off talking about potatoes, potholders, and penguins. At one point, I wrote, "It's nothing to be a singer or a dancer or an actor. The thing is jugglers." I used to underestimate them until I saw a pair of juggling brothers—the timing, the discipline, the precision, the imagination, their sense of humor! They were brilliant.

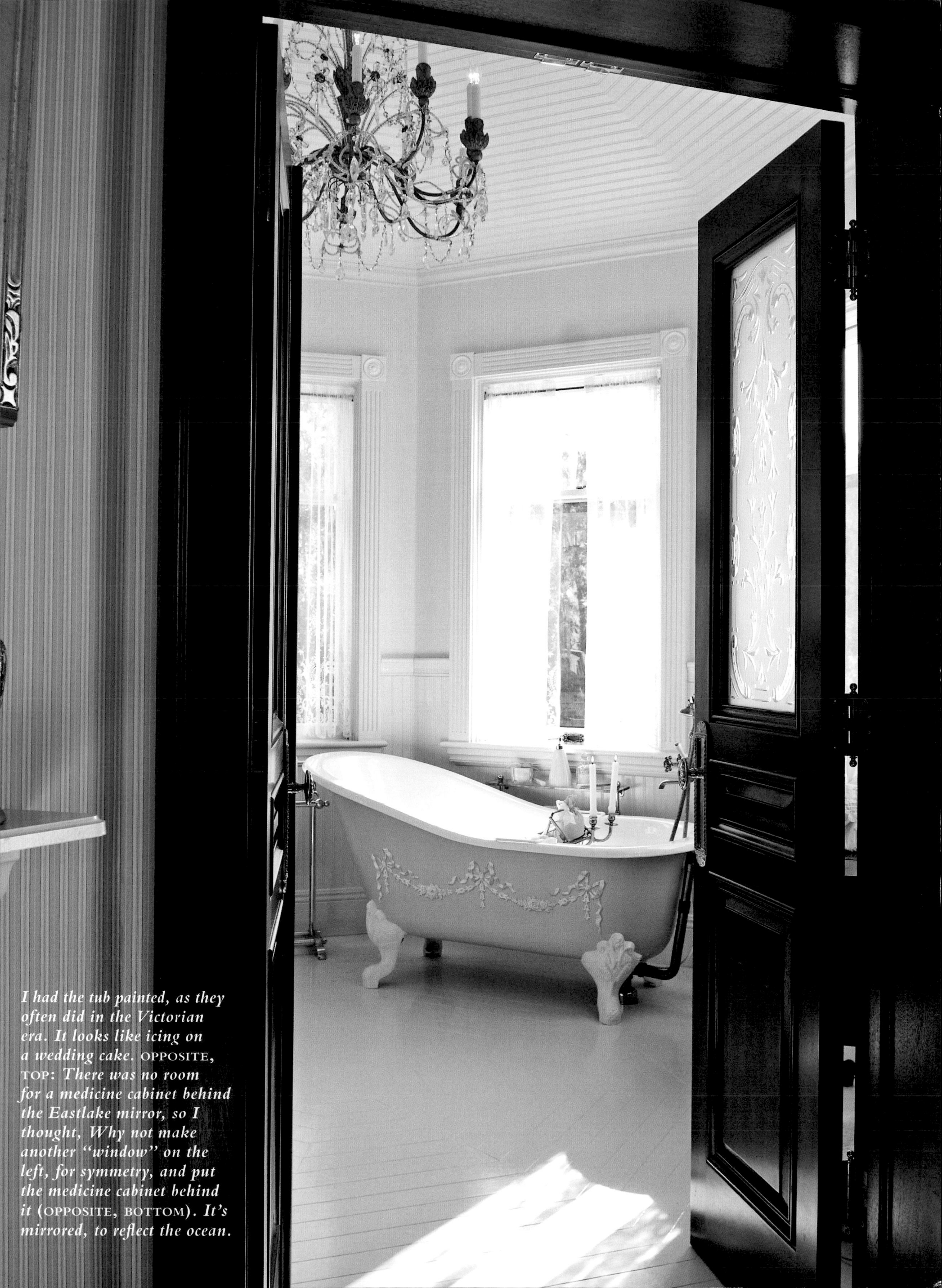

I had the tub painted, as they often did in the Victorian era. It looks like icing on a wedding cake. OPPOSITE, TOP: *There was no room for a medicine cabinet behind the Eastlake mirror, so I thought, Why not make another "window" on the left, for symmetry, and put the medicine cabinet behind it* (OPPOSITE, BOTTOM). *It's mirrored, to reflect the ocean.*

A Room with a View

When we built this storage space, I was thinking of something along the lines of a fine men's clothing shop in London, the kind with mahogany paneling and a tailor who appears to take your measurements. And just like in those shops, you don't immediately see any clothes.

We had a hard time with those straw inserts on the chests of drawers. It was raining outside when they glued them on, and they all buckled. So they had to be redone. Then the stain started to come off... Let's change the subject.

I hardly ever shop anymore. I don't have the time or the inclination. Either Renata finds me comfortable clothes or I design some formal things for myself, and I still wear my antique bits. My good friend Donna Karan also sends me things and I buy what works. I love her and her clothes, because we both believe in comfort—elastic waists, wide sweaters ... clothes for eating. ❧

ABOVE: *The two mirrored cabinets in the walk-in closet are designed to resemble antique armoires. The chests have a woven straw insert on all the drawers, which creates that two-toned effect I love, with the lighter straw against the darker wood. And of course the straw had to be a certain color, with just the right amount of red in the stain. The little loveseat came from my Carolwood house and gives you a place to sit and put on your shoes.*
OPPOSITE: *A window with lace curtains frames a view of the mill house. Everything looks better through lace.*

In an old New England farmhouse, the boards in the wainscoting on either side of a doorway don't match. They're different sizes. Clearly they just used what they had on hand. It's very unpretentious.

The Blue Bathroom

I was visiting my friends Diana and Gary David Goldberg up at their 18th-century dairy farm in Vermont and couldn't get over the beauty of those simple farmhouse rooms. The wood paneling in this particular room seemed to be placed almost randomly on the walls, and it ran horizontally rather than vertically, which I thought was so unique. I decided to do my own version in this little powder room.

I already had the old wood. Originally, I bought it for the panels in the great room, but it was too crude. I wanted a rich, honey-colored look in there and in order to get it, the wood had to be smoother, with the right amount of knots—not too many and not too few.

Vicente put up the boards himself. Now we needed a sink. I asked Kim Skalecki, who was my secretary at the time (and was with me for over 30 years), and my son, Jason, if they would like to go to Brimfield in Massachusetts. They both love antiquing, so I thought it might be fun for them. This is one of the great country fairs—the dealers set up their stalls in the middle of the fields. The two of them traipsed around in the wet mud looking for dry sinks and came back with just what I wanted. There's something very appealing about those big, bathtub-size sinks. I decided to put blue slate on top of the old wooden cabinet, and went to various stone yards to find just the right shade. The design in the wallpaper looks old and faded, even though it's new. Last touch—traveling around New England, I found various early American samplers that were embroidered in those same dusty blues.

ABOVE: *The image of this 18th-century farmhouse door with iron hinges was embedded in my brain for many years.* OPPOSITE: *So our bathroom door was modeled after it* (BOTTOM, RIGHT). *The outside* (BOTTOM, LEFT) *has different hardware and wood, to match a more formal hallway. This is the 18th-century room* (TOP, LEFT) *that inspired my powder room* (TOP, RIGHT). *Vicente made that mirror and lined the frame with leftover pieces of slate. He's so good!*

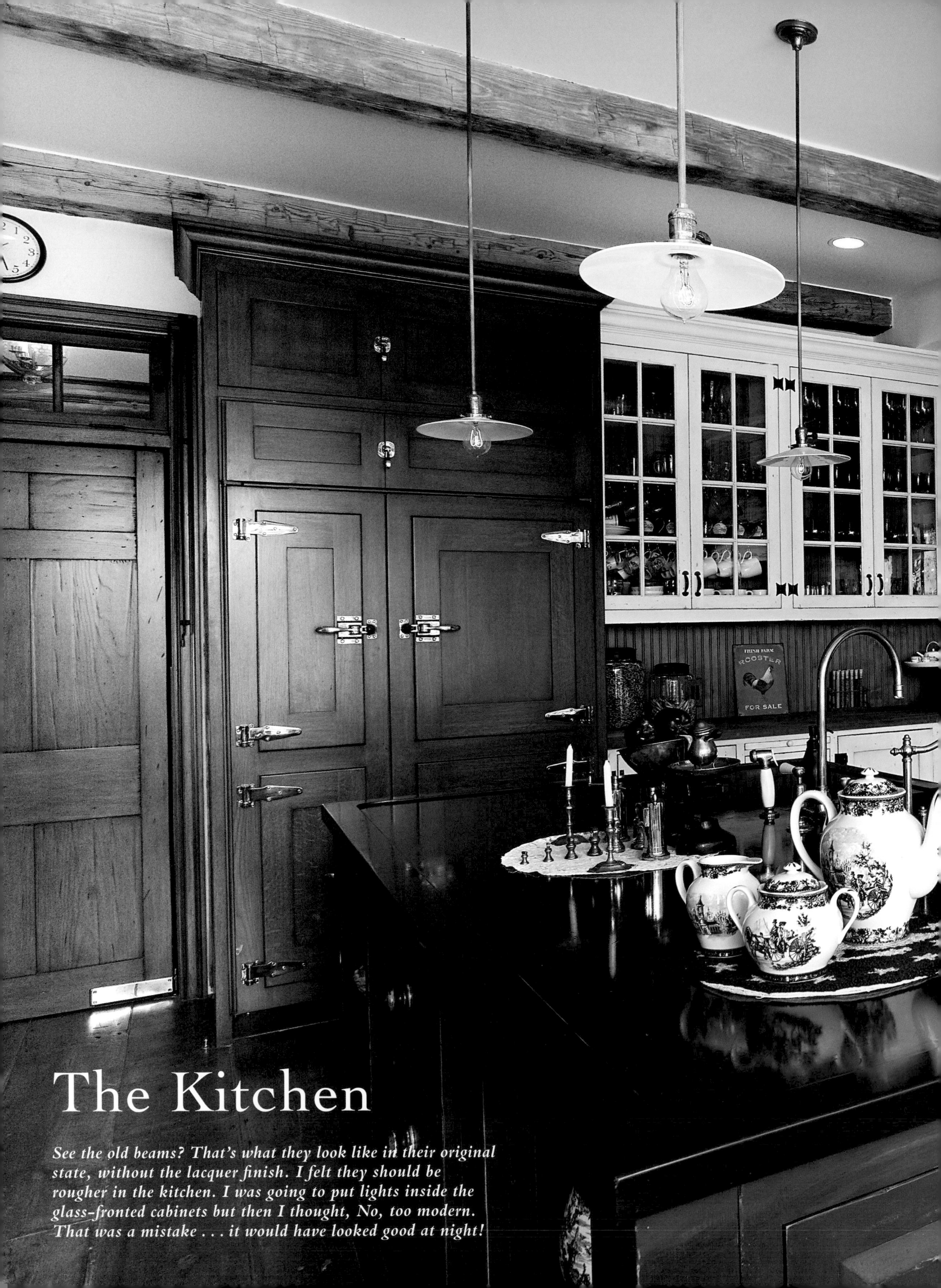

The Kitchen

See the old beams? That's what they look like in their original state, without the lacquer finish. I felt they should be rougher in the kitchen. I was going to put lights inside the glass-fronted cabinets but then I thought, No, too modern. That was a mistake . . . it would have looked good at night!

20
EGGS
15 ¢ DOZ.

This is my farmhouse kitchen. It feels warm and homey, as if you were just about to take a pie out of the oven and put it on the windowsill to cool. The whole room seems to belong to a kinder, gentler era. The countertops are cherry, like you'd see in a turn-of-the-last-century house in New England. The refrigerator looks like an old-fashioned icebox with big brass hinges. That was another challenge. Nobody makes hinges like that anymore. The new stuff is too little. We finally found a guy who said he could make them. But I had to wait two years before he finally produced anything. He was an artist, I guess. Thank god the house took so long to build.

The kitchen cabinets are simple and utilitarian, painted an old, warm white. I had a great painter (expensive, but worth it) and took him over to Grandma's house to see my old painted hutches and chests. I gave him a drawer so he could study the paint and have it right beside him while he worked. He did a brilliant job.

Last summer I was out in East Hampton, and I went through one of those just-built Shingle-style houses by a well-known architect. I was so surprised—everything looked too new. The paint was too perfect! You need a few artful scratches and streaks and worn-off spots to look authentic.

I wanted this house to feel old in a beautiful (not run-down) way. But that may be my own quirkiness. Other people want their houses to look nice and new. They don't want to age the paint or put a few dents in the cabinetry. But I come from the movie world, where the challenge is to make it look as if it had been standing there for a century or two.

The counters are all wood but I wasn't sure what to put on top of the island. I love wood, but it's not very practical when you're washing vegetables and chopping them or washing dishes. Soapstone could be right. It's practically indestructible, and it suits the period. I bought this huge slab of dark green soapstone that they promised me would turn black after a few coats of mineral oil. I even had a custom sink made out of the stuff. But it never looked black enough. It was still dark green to my eye. So I opted for slate instead. I wanted that rich off-black against the off-white cabinets. I've recently started to collect old black and white transferware. It looks so pretty when we eat outside—I like seeing those dishes against the black and off-white exterior of the house.

You have to have a place to sit in a kitchen. This little table (ABOVE), with three Windsor chairs, feels even cozier in the lamplight. The antique wooden bucket by the door (it's called a firkin) probably once held butter or lard. Now we use it as a wastebasket. OPPOSITE: Here, the pass-through to the great room is open. The bin drawers look like something you'd see in an old general store. Those dishes in the rack have waterwheels on them—a lovely present from Kim.

25 OUNCES FOR 25¢
BUTTER-EGGS
Cook And Bake With
KC
BAKING POWDER
69
CENTS
KC
25
Chesterfield

The Black Bathroom

The bathroom was built around that beautiful reverse-painted lamp made by the Jefferson Lamp Co. of Chicago, probably around 1910. It has roses on a black background, so you can imagine how thrilled I was to find that wallpaper. But what should the proportion of wallpaper to wainscoting be? I asked my draftsman to draw the chair rail at several heights. Then we made a mock-up so I could stand in the room and see how it would feel. I've had those two clocks with that pretty mother-of-pearl detailing for years. I think I found them in Paris. I used to go over to France when I was collecting Art Nouveau and Art Deco and send a container back to the States, filled with all sorts of things from the shops and flea markets. The Victorian sewing table, the two chairs, and the étagère are all black-lacquered papier-mâché furniture inlaid with mother-of-pearl. When I was playing Daisy in *On a Clear Day You Can See Forever*, I collected things with daisies on them and one was a writing tablet made of the same stuff. I just gave it to the little girl who played my granddaughter in *Little Fockers*, because her name is Daisy. She seemed delighted with her first antique piece … that's how a collector is born. ❧

ABOVE: *When I saw that painted cabinet, in the same odd mustard green as the leaves in the wallpaper, I knew it was meant for this room. We cut a hole in the top and I had a black matte sink custom made to match the black matte wallpaper and the lamp base.* OPPOSITE: *I decided to do the ceiling in the same honey-colored beadboard as the wainscoting. It makes the room feel cozy.*

Underground . . . a Basement?? . . . No . . . a Street.

At first I planned to use the basement as a storage room for antiques so I could stop paying all those fees to storage companies. But then I thought, How ridiculous. If I still haven't got a place for something after building this house, I should let it go. Pass it on and let someone else enjoy it. So I sent a lot of things off to be sold at auction.

Besides, I had another idea for this space. Why not do a street of shops like I had seen at Winterthur? In one section of the museum, they recreated all these little stores . . . a china shop, a country store . . . just the way they would have looked in the early 1800s. And then they used them to display various collections. Wouldn't it be fun to do something similar?

I could use all exterior materials on the storefronts . . . clapboard and shingle in shades of white . . . brick . . . as well as some rich brown wood. I was thinking of doing one shop in stone, but we were having a hard time finding just the right off-white color. Meanwhile, on a trip back east, I visited the Peabody Essex Museum in Salem, Massachusetts, which had an 18th-century door on display, with two pieces of the surrounding wall. I looked at this stone wall from the real house, and then came closer and touched it. The "stone" was actually made out of

TOP: *When you come down the silo staircase, the first shop on the right, with the bay window, is my doll shop.* BOTTOM: *The park bench is a place for the guys to park themselves while the girls look at the dolls.* OPPOSITE: *Alan Jergens, my movie painter, did an excellent job on the faux-stone walls, concocting a lovely cream color that blends right in with the Charente stone from France on the floor. The street is lit with outdoor lanterns.*

& GENTS
ON HALL
EDLER'S
Lithographic Printer.
FIRST FLOOR.
VILLA
Phone: Battersea
SAWYER & S
BUILDER'S & DECOR
Office at 152A Earlsfield
EARLSFIELD. S
and at 58, Brocklebank
Maintenance work a SPECIA
VICTORIA
SILK
ASSOCIATION

wood and just faux painted. Immediately, I called John and said, "We're doing it out of wood. I don't want the stone. I want what they did in the 18th century."

And then I threw in a little something from *Meet the Fockers*. The dark paneled doors with those lovely posts and corbels were originally part of the *Fockers* set. I asked Rusty Smith, the production designer, "What are you going to do with those doors when we're done?" He said, "Throw them out." I said, "I'll take them." I hate waste, I needed doors, and they felt as if they belonged here. In fact, those corbels were inspired by a picture I had given him of rocking chairs on a porch with that same detail. Rusty had looked through my research files, because at that point I was in the planning stages for this house and hoping he

would help me draw up the design. Somehow, it's appropriate that they found their way back here.

Unfortunately, the doors were cheaply made (no wonder, since they were only meant to last a few weeks), and it probably cost more to take them apart and reglue them than it would have cost to make them from scratch. But the big attraction for me was that they were already done. I could put them up and worry about them falling apart later.

ABOVE: *Robert Shachtman did the drawing for the storefronts, designed around the doors from the* Meet the Fockers *set.* LEFT AND RIGHT: *He also did a wonderful job on the drawings for the period signage on the glass transoms, and Andreas Lehmann executed them beautifully.*

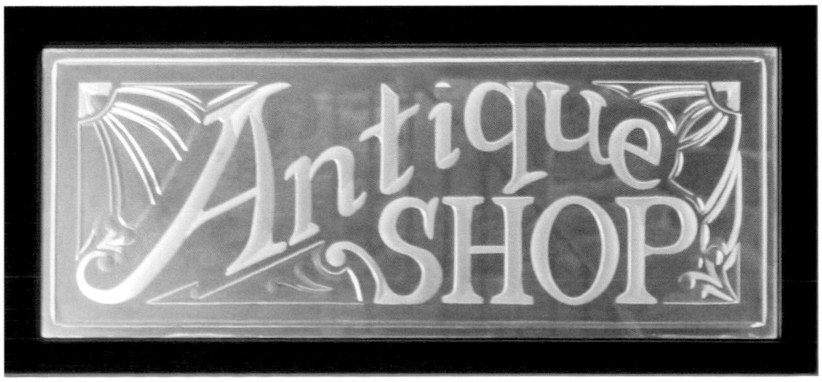

Bee's Doll Shop

I never played with dolls as a child because I didn't have any. I used to fill a hot water bottle with warm water and pretend it was a baby. Toby, the neighbor who took care of me, knitted me a little pink hat and a little pink sweater for it. When you don't have things, you learn to use your imagination.

Then in 1987, when I came to look at the house that is now my main house—although I didn't buy it then—I saw the owner's doll collection. I had never really paid attention to antique dolls before and I was suddenly besotted with them. I think it was the clothes that first caught my eye, with all the minute details . . . the pleating . . . the buttons . . . the little lace trims. How did they make ribbon an eighth of an inch wide? And then I was entranced with the porcelain faces . . . the wide eyes . . . the delicately painted eyebrows . . . the tiny teeth. I doubt children ever played with these. They're so fragile. You drop one and it will break.

I started buying dolls at auction, ordering all the catalogues from Christie's and Sotheby's. Soon I was bidding on Jumeau and Bru dolls in London and Paris. I would go to an antiques show and come back with one or two that I felt a rapport with. I do love some more than others because they're unusual or rare, like my long-faced doll with her pensive, almost sad expression. French automatons fascinate me—you wind them up and they move and do things, such as iron a dress or serve tea. I bought classic French bébé dolls that look like infants and sophisticated French fashion dolls modeling the most exquisite clothes. And I also collect antique black dolls, which carry so much emotion.

I have two doll buddies, Michael Canadas and David Robinson, who own the Carmel Doll Shop, where I buy lots of things. The three of us have gone on shopping trips everywhere from Pasadena to Paris, where they've taken me to meet other dealers who work out of their homes. Sometimes I'll buy a doll with a great face and a great history, but her clothes will be ruined. Then Michael, who is the best doll couturier around, will whip up a gorgeous outfit for her with delicate pin tucks and ruching.

The dolls themselves are only the beginning. Naturally, you need chairs for them to sit in . . . doll beds . . . doll carriages. And you have to have all the accessories to go with the clothes, like little hankies and hats and parasols. The accoutrements are endless, which is part of the fun.

Now imagine all that in miniature, and you'll understand the allure of dollhouses for me. I never had one as a child and by the way, if I did see any back then, they would have been made of tin with plastic furniture. Plastic didn't interest me. I never really saw antique dollhouses until I walked into a little museum of miniatures that used to be across the street from the Los Angeles

A miniature antique storefront I found in England inspired the arched door to the doll shop. Each ceiling in each store is different. Here, the pressed tiles are made of brass to match the hardware. OPPOSITE: *A sign painter did the lettering.*

ETRENNES
Café

Look at the doll holding a pipe on the shelf to the left. She's a French automaton, and when you wind her up, she blows bubbles. Her friend at the other end of the shelf, sitting on a chair, is also an automaton. She knits. I knew I wanted to put that dollhouse in the bay window, so we made sure the window was just the right size for it.

ABOVE, LEFT: *The Captain's House is modeled after an old Nantucket home, complete with widow's walk.* ABOVE, RIGHT: *You can tell this is mine—burgundy curtains, and every table is set for tea.* BELOW: *This late Georgian dollhouse dates back to 1840 and once belonged to Graham Greene's wife, Vivien, who was a major collector. The exterior is scored to look like stone.* OPPOSITE: *It came with only a few pieces, like the artist's model . . . very bohemian . . . and I furnished it with the help of my doll buddies. While the husband is laboring over his canvas with his miniature palette and tiny tubes of paint, his wife in the room across the hall has just given birth to a baby. The doctor with his black bag is still there.*

County Museum of Art. I was overwhelmed. What is it about miniatures? I find them so enchanting. It's an entire world that's complete in every detail, yet so tiny. Imagine a silver tea set with a toast rack . . . a chest of drawers . . . playing cards . . . sized for dolls just six inches tall.

Michael and David come over every so often, and we work on my dollhouses. It's the perfect pastime for someone like me who loves decorating rooms because I can keep going even though I've run out of real rooms to decorate . . . and best of all, it involves *no contractors*!!! David is a genius at renovating dollhouses. He can repair moldings and put up new wallpaper and wire them for electricity. And Michael will make bedspreads and curtains. We each get completely immersed in the process.

Every September a little dollhouse museum in Santa Monica called Angels Attic has a big sale, and we all go. One year, I got a great buy on a large selection of miniature food. (I love food in all its forms, if you haven't already noticed.) Even David and Michael were impressed. "Where did you find that?" they asked. "We didn't see it." Now my dollhouse families eat very well.

See why I liked those corbels? They add an interesting architectural element to the street. The Sweet Shop gets a lot of traffic when we're screening a movie. OPPOSITE: *Would you like some licorice? How about some jelly beans? There's also frozen yogurt. One of the flavors is usually coffee, my favorite. And of course you have to have a popcorn machine.*

Sweet Shop

This is the Antique Shop, for leftover things I couldn't part with. I bought the white iron daybed for my stepdaughter Molly's room in the main house, when she was a little girl. The doll bed belongs to Sammie. Every year on her birthday, she gets a lovely piece of furniture from my friend Sue Balmforth at Bountiful Antiques. Sue introduced me to Sammie's breed and has several Cotons de Tuléar of her own. I love that wallpaper by Farrow & Ball and used it in different colors in different stores. (You can do that when it's your own mall!)

I bought that fireplace when I was in my chalk-white period. The photograph of me, holding my cherished Sadie, was taken while I was in Funny Girl. OPPOSITE, CLOCKWISE, FROM TOP LEFT: *Lace curtains hang in the windows of the Antique Shop. Elliott Gould, my former husband, found that dog portrait and brought it to me in the hospital when our son, Jason, was born. I found an old French sink at Sue's place and had the side cabinets made for it. This is an English house, in miniature.*

Antique
SHOP

americana
ANTIQUES
for sale

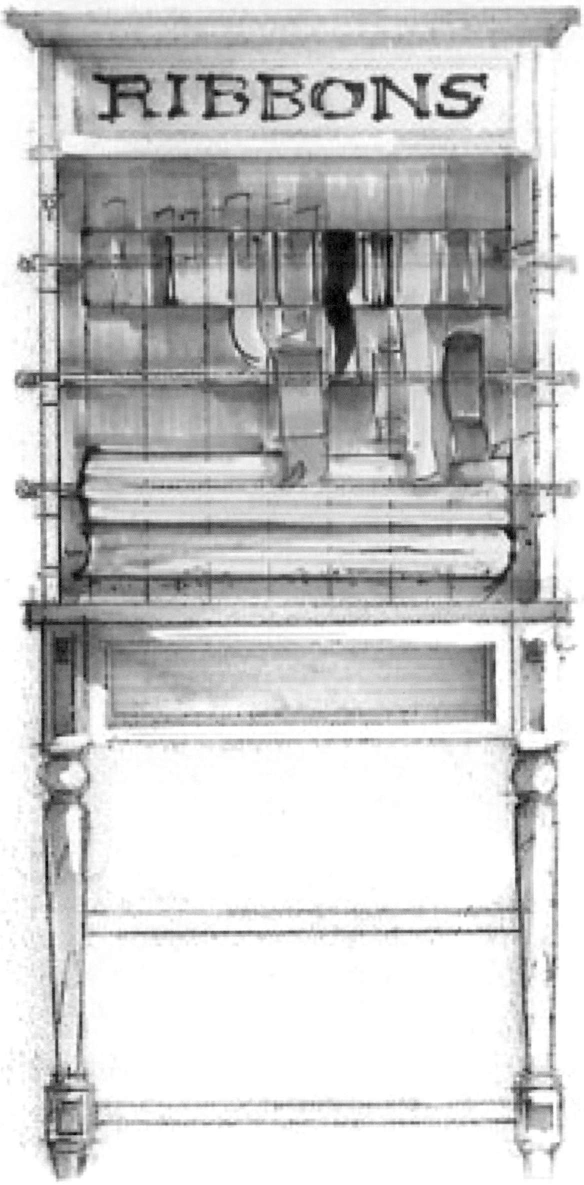

ABOVE, LEFT: *This is a table for wrapping presents. It seems like every week someone we know has a birthday.* ABOVE, RIGHT: *I told my draftsman Dwight Jackson what I had in mind, and he did a very good job drawing it up. I love beautiful ribbons and wanted to be able to see them.* OPPOSITE: *This corner piece with the seat and the shelves is one unit. It used to be in my Carolwood house, upholstered in blue and white stripes, and I had it recovered for this room. And here's that Farrow & Ball wallpaper again, this time in apple green.*

The Gift Shoppe

Before I go out to a friend's house for a dinner party, I'll often come down to my Gift Shoppe. I like to bring people a present, something that will last longer than flowers. The cupboards in here are filled with things that I love . . . antique dishes that could hold a bar of soap . . . pretty candlesticks . . . Arts & Crafts pottery . . . all kinds of treasures. I'll look through the stash and see if I can find something that would suit my host. I like the idea of passing things on.

The Root Cellar

I call this room my root cellar because it really is for the flowers and fruits and vegetables we want to keep fresh. That's why we built the walk-in refrigerator, to take the overflow from the garden. The flowers for the house are also arranged right here in an old dry sink, which I lined in stainless steel and fitted with running water. The room also serves as an auxiliary kitchen. I didn't have room for a wall oven upstairs, so we put one down here.

It's also a place for a washer and dryer. Unfortunately the room took so long to build that when I was finally ready to install the ones I had picked out, the models were discontinued. So then I had to change the design to accommodate a stacked unit that we hid behind a door, and it's actually better that way. Just beyond the sink, there's a closet for things that have to drip-dry. I love great tile work . . . the details on the fish and game tiles and the molded backsplash tiles are so well done. ❧

AQUAFINA

The Antique Clothes Shop

I was 16 years old when I discovered thrift shops and fell in love with antique clothing . . . 1920s velvet dresses with lace collars . . . a watery taffeta cape with scalloped edges . . . 1940s coats with sequined trims on the shoulders. I had never seen anything so beautiful. The cut, the fabrics, and the workmanship were all infinitely better than what was available in regular department stores. And these wonderful old clothes were even less expensive!

I wore antique clothing the first time I ever sang professionally, at a Greenwich Village nightclub called the Bon Soir. I was 18 years old and had never even been in a nightclub before I sang in one. I found a high-necked black velvet bodice that laced up in the back and had a black velvet skirt made. I remember the bodice was embroidered with steel-cut black beads that caught the light. And I finished off this ensemble with a pair of antique shoes with black and silver buckles. They had hardly been worn, yet by the end of the evening the leather inside was completely burned out, just from the heat of my body. I still have them. (Unfortunately the black bodice was lost in a basement flood.)

But then the press started talking about my clothes as if they were a gimmick. I thought, Oh no! I never meant them to be distracting. So I went back to the thrift shops and bought very simple dresses. I also began designing my own outfits to wear onstage—full-length slit skirts with vests made out of herringbone or pinstriped wool, which I paired with soft chiffon blouses. (There's that dichotomy again.) It's on the cover of my first album. But I never stopped wearing antique clothes in private. In fact, I've worn practically everything in this closet, except for the dresses that date back to the Civil War! Hard to get around in hoop skirts these days!

I thought this room would be an opportunity to get my things out of storage and display some of my favorite pieces. At first, I had the woodwork painted to match the color of a Butterscotch rose as it was fading . . . with off-white trim. And then after it was all done, I thought, You know what? The root cellar is going to be golden yellow—too similar. What other color could I do?

I've always loved lavender . . . I'll do a lavender room. I wanted to use only colors I love in this house, and there aren't that many of them. (I couldn't live with orange, or royal blue, or dark purple.) Thank goodness I have no more rooms, because I would run out of colors.

This room was still under construction in 2007 when I had to leave for Europe on my concert tour. In Vienna I saw the most beautiful herringbone floor in one of the palaces. I measured the width of the boards and sent pictures back to my crew, telling them that this was how I wanted the floor to

I found the chaise while I was antiquing in the Loire Valley in between shows on my European concert tour and had it recovered in lavender velvet. In the showcase on the left is a crepe silk dress that Cecil Beaton designed for that big dining room scene in On a Clear Day You Can See Forever. *It's embroidered with thousands of tiny pearls, rhinestones, and iridescent sequins. I asked Ray Aghayan to make that lavender velvet cape for me, with Art Nouveau beading down the back. I wore it to meet the Queen of England at the opening of* Funny Lady *in London.*

look in this room. What palace was that? It's famous. I sang in front of it. Oh god, this is terrible. And it's not age. I never know where I am. I've lived in London several times but I couldn't tell you where unless I looked it up. Years ago, Steven Spielberg and I would get lost trying to find a street in Beverly Hills, where we lived! No kidding. He was one of the first people I know to get a GPS system. Actually, it was even before GPS . . . some gizmo called E-Tac. I remember the day when he called me up, so excited to show it to me. Being a director clearly has nothing to do with having a sense of direction. When I was directing *Yentl* at Lee International Studios in London, I was always going the wrong way back to my dressing room, so the crew kindly put yellow tape on the floor so I could follow it.

LEFT: *This was an early idea for the room, but the concept changed after I found that 18th-century chaise and the Aubusson rug. It was hard to give up my ottomans because they were going to be so pretty, but I was able to use some of the fabrics and trims on the pillows and the chairs.* ABOVE: *My inexpensive eBay chairs look a lot better in antique gold and lavender velvet. By the way, I'm still looking for real period pieces. The cabinet drawers hold bits of antique lace, ribbon, and things like that.* OPPOSITE: *The mirrored closets reflect a French chandelier I bought in 1964 for my New York apartment. I love how the bronze arms are entwined with porcelain flowers. More recently, I found a pair in London that were similar and hung them on either side of the original.*

The Schönbrunn Palace! That's it. That's where I saw all this incredible gold detailing on the woodwork and the herringbone floor with three-and-one-half-inch-wide boards. (Measurements, I remember.) I thought it would be perfect in my room, with a darker wood border. I was going to do a French table in the center, with a big round ottoman at each end, and I was planning to have a rug woven with flowers. But then while I was in London on the last leg of the tour I walked into one of my favorite stores, C. John. They have the most beautiful rugs. I said, "I know this is probably improbable, but do you happen to have anything with a lavender background?" And they pulled out a beautiful Aubusson, in lavender, with the most subtle rose, green, and gold accents. That was very exciting. I'll take it! Then I don't have to wait eight months for the other rug to be made. And since the Aubusson is too pretty to hide, let's forget the table and the ottomans. (The room was a little narrow for a table, anyway.) I'll buy that 18th-century chaise I saw in France and put it at one end of the room, with two chairs that I

OVERLEAF, LEFT: *I wore the black dress with the white feathered muff and the tall black hat, another Cecil Beaton ensemble, in* On a Clear Day You Can See Forever. *In 1963 President John F. Kennedy invited me to sing at the White House Correspondents dinner. I designed a modern version of a silk Empire dress for the occasion and had it made in gray wool with buttons that went from small to large down the front. I love the look of a middy blouse and designed several versions—they gave me room to breathe when I sang. I wore one on Judy Garland's show that same year.* OVERLEAF, RIGHT: *I like all these fine laces and cottons and silks . . . dresses . . . robes . . . combing jackets. All in pastel shades—pink, peach, and off-white. P.S. I bought the lavender robe of ruffles when I was pregnant with my son, Jason.*

got on eBay for $500 at the other. They were an ugly brown, and I had my finisher, Ricky Jimenez, redo them in the same gold to match the antique chaise. Suddenly, the room came together. It was simpler and more elegant. And the focus was where it belonged—on the clothing.

In the 1960s I used to be a clotheshorse . . . I attended fashion shows in Paris . . . wore Dior. Now I dress very simply. In other words, I always wear the same thing, which you can probably tell from my photos. I'm usually in black . . . a black top, a black sweater, black pants. I just don't have time to shop! And by the way, when I *do* go shopping (once or twice a year) I somehow end up buying the same things all over again.

ABOVE, LEFT: *That violet silk velvet dress is one of the first antique pieces I ever bought. It's so nice to touch.* ABOVE, RIGHT: *I bought this 1930s coat for $10 and wore it to the audition for* I Can Get It for You Wholesale *because it was a 1930s play. It's made of caracal fur with a fox trim. It's an extraordinary color, but what I really loved about it was that the inside was as beautiful as the outside. I couldn't believe that the lining was embroidered with all those chenille flowers. Very few people would ever see it, but they did it anyway. I asked Irene Sharaff, the costume designer for* Funny Girl, *to copy it in off-white so I could wear it onstage because I had read that off-white was Fanny Brice's favorite color.* LEFT: *I'm fascinated with beaded leather shoes, here in black, gold, and bronze. Imagine pushing a tiny needle through leather. Not easy.*

I sang "People" in this dress in the stage version of **Funny Girl**. *Irene Sharaff designed it in green chiffon over pink silk, with little beaded balls on the sleeves . . . quirky, like the character. She did a slightly more elaborate version for the movie. But this is the one I prefer.*

I thought the Fortuny dress was gorgeous. Utterly simple—held together by a thin silk cord at the shoulders . . . and very complex—with that infinitesimal pleating.

Aesthetically, I would prefer wearing period clothes. I love the look of Napoleonic Empire dresses, bustles, Paul Poiret's "Persian" fantasies from the 1920s. But since the styles today don't interest me much, I might as well be physically comfortable, you know what I mean? Elastic waists . . . stretch fabrics. I still love lace collars and things. If I have to get dressed up, I'll often wear some of my vintage pieces with a new suit or dress, as I did for the 2010 Oscars ceremony. I had some antique lace scarves turned into a blouse and wore it with a black jacket and a long slit skirt. I wouldn't mind wearing one of those beautiful haute couture gowns, but you have to find it, first of all, and then have umpteen fittings, and it takes so much time! These days, I have other priorities.

OPPOSITE: *Irene Sharaff found the Fortuny dress for me. No one has ever figured out how he did those tiny pleats. It's like Tiffany glass in a way. You can't quite duplicate it, although many people have tried. I wore the original in the movie of* Funny Girl (ABOVE) *and then I had Irene copy it in pink for my 1967 concert in Central Park. I asked her to make a pleated chiffon cape to wear over it that could billow in the wind. There were 150,000 people there that night and no video screens back then. At least with the cape, they could see me, even if they were way in the back.*

The Georgian Display Room

I couldn't resist one last octagon. The geometry of the room seems to suit the precision of the Georgian architecture. And then there's an unpredictable mix of things on the shelves. If you look closely, you'll see 18th-century creamware and Art Nouveau plates trimmed with green . . . a Wiener Werkstätte tea set . . . Art Nouveau champagne glasses that I bought from Lillian Nassau when I was 22 years old . . . a great Teco vase . . . delicately beaded fans . . . pictures of my friends and my son, Jason, in Art Nouveau frames. There are objects here that I bought when I was a teenager. I should have been a curator. I love arranging things.

What holds it all together are the touches of green. The Tiffany candlesticks on the shelf have green glass shades. The 19th-century Chippendale chairs are upholstered in green damask, and I recently added the nailhead trim. Green is the color that runs through the room and the various collections. I suppose you could call this a glorified butler's pantry. It's a quiet room, a place where you could sit and study an object. There are reference books in the lower cupboards. I like learning about all these diverse and beautiful things.

LEFT: *Jack Taylor, the art director, did the drawings for this room after I told him what I envisioned. Movie people are accustomed to doing lots of research, which shows in the detail of this door.* OPPOSITE: *When I walked into an antiques shop in Atlanta and saw that octagonal display table, my jaw dropped. It was perfect for this room!*

The Art Nouveau Rooms

At the end of the street of shops, you go through a door and suddenly you're in Paris in 1904, with sinuous Art Nouveau woodwork and a rich green tone-on-tone Art Nouveau paper on the walls. I've had the posters of Sarah Bernhardt by Alphonse Mucha for many, many years. When I was 16 I used to spend a lot of time at the New York Public Library on 42nd Street, looking up all the plays she was in. I identified with her because she was Jewish on her mother's side. Most people have no idea that she was also an accomplished painter and sculptor who exhibited her work in Paris, London, and New York. She did too many things too well, which annoyed some critics. They assumed that she must have had someone else do the sculpting for her, which was totally untrue.

Bernhardt had a very good eye. Mucha was an unknown artist in 1894 when she picked a poster he had done, on spec, to promote her latest play. The printer was reluctant even to show it to her, because the style was so unconventional.

TOP: *That odd chair still had its original Art Nouveau fabric, so I couldn't pass it up.* LEFT: *Bernhardt made this sculpture. The way she saw herself, with bat wings, claw-like hands, and a griffon's tail, was intriguing to me. I was thrilled to see another casting of it recently in the Boston Museum of Fine Arts.* OPPOSITE: *I found the hall tree in Brussels.* OVERLEAF, LEFT: *I had this piece of Art Nouveau leaded glass tucked away for years and then had the door built around it. Straight ahead is the Emile Gallé cabinet, with blossoms of Queen Anne's lace carved in relief along the top. I love how he used the curve of the stem to make an arch across the front.* OVERLEAF, RIGHT: *Louis Majorelle designed these chairs, and Sarah Bernhardt also owned at least one. The table is by Gallé and the fireplace, which looks like wood although it's made of embossed metal, is by Majorelle. If you look carefully, you can see how the center motif of the leaded glass in the door inspired the carving on the crown moldings.*

LORENZACCIO
SARAH BERNHARDT

But Bernhardt loved it and began an artistic collaboration with Mucha that lasted for years. In addition to posters, he also designed sets, costumes, and jewelry for her.

There was another architect who belonged in this house if it was going to represent the best of 1904—Hector Guimard. You know his work if you've ever seen one of those fabulous Paris Metro stations that are now icons of Art Nouveau. I still own several pieces of his—a delicately carved pearwood mirror and an unusual chandelier made of long, thin crystal rods that cast the most extraordinary pattern on the ceiling. That's the key to Guimard: He was amazingly inventive. When I sold most of my collection of Art Nouveau at Christie's in 1994, I held these items back. I just couldn't let them go.

LEFT: *I had the sconces electrified and added a mahogany back plate.* ABOVE, LEFT: *I found the upholstery fabric for the settees in Paris after a dealer at a flea market gave me a great source for Art Nouveau fabric. Would you believe it's printed with* ombelles, *and it came in peach and green . . . exactly my colors.* ABOVE, RIGHT: *When I bought those two Majorelle chairs in the 1960s, I didn't even know who Majorelle was. I had them covered in green velvet, which still works very well here. Doesn't the Guimard chandelier cast a beautiful pattern of light on the ceiling?*

What is it about Art Nouveau? It's such a part of my psyche by now that it's hard to explain why I love it. Maybe I once lived at that time . . . or maybe I *should* have lived at that time. I don't know. But there is something very feminine about those flowing lines . . . the soft, round curves . . . the opposite of the straight-lined simplicity of Stickley. It has a sensual quality.

In fact, my first concept for this room involved a kind of bed in the center, with a low headboard so you could sit, surrounded by pillows, facing the fireplace. But you can't light the fire because there's no flue. And no drawing looked right. So I said, Let's just make a sofa out of this beautiful silk velvet in a gorgeous peach color. And you know what? It's fine. It actually opens up the space. And once I moved that original 1905 Charles F. A. Voysey rug down from the Mackintosh Hall, where it didn't quite fit, it seemed as if it was meant to be here. The color in the rug is the same color that's on the walls. It's a peach with umber in it, which gives it some age . . . as if men had talked and smoked cigars in this room for years and the smoke had penetrated the paint.

ABOVE: *Art Nouveau is about grace and fluidity. Everything curves like the stem of a plant bending in the wind, and you see that in the organic lines of the woodwork in this room. I once owned the matching settee to my Majorelle armchairs, but I sold it at auction (not my smartest move). Since I wanted one place to sit that was really comfortable, I went with this sofa. It's covered in peach silk velvet with a peach and green tasseled fringe. The pillows are made from remnants of original Art Nouveau fabric. It's cozy, but I keep looking through auction catalogues . . . maybe my Majorelle settee will show up one day.*

The two chairs in the center of the room are by Louis Majorelle. When I saw them in Paris in the early 1970s, I was immediately drawn to them. Twenty years later I was looking through a book on Sarah Bernhardt and there were two pieces of her furniture pictured in it, one of which was this chair. Isn't that unbelievable? So she and I share the same taste. The chairs are covered in the original fabric, embroidered with *ombelles,* the French name for Queen Anne's lace. For some reason, this particular flower became a favorite Art Nouveau motif. It's carved into the wood of these chairs and the table between them. It's also incorporated into the design of the wooden vitrine by Emile Gallé. How imaginative to carve shelves as if they were the heads of flowers supported by a stem. I thought it was stunning when I saw it at Lillian Nassau's shop in New York when I was 22 years old, and had to save up to buy it.

One of the most satisfying things about building this room was that I would finally have a place for my very tall and rather commanding corner settee, which had languished in storage for decades. There was just one problem. You know how I appreciate symmetry. It was too off-balance to have just one standing in the right-hand corner. I had to complete the wall. So I had the mirror image made for the left-hand corner.

Lighting can be so magical . . . like my Guimard chandelier, which made a plain plaster ceiling look like gathered fabric, a lovely illusion. I also had two wonderful Gallé sconces (which I had pulled out of my auction at the last minute). I placed them on either side of the Guimard mirror over the fireplace. But the room needed more light. When I was in London on my European tour, I dropped by Denton Antiques, where I've been buying chandeliers for years, and there on the wall was the perfect pair of authentic Art Nouveau bronze sconces. "Oh my god, that's exactly what I want. Problem is, I need six of them," I told the salesman. "Maybe I could have them copied." He smiled and said, "That won't be necessary. I have four more in the back." I couldn't believe he had a set, in just the right number. That's serendipity.

The Art Nouveau Bathroom

When I like something, I tend to like it forever (except for Art Deco, but that's another story, and I think I'll save it for Volume II). I had the Art Nouveau vanity and mirror made for my Carolwood home 30 years ago. When I sold the house, I said to the buyer, "If you're not going to keep this sink, I'd like it back." And he let me remove it. It fits perfectly here. Imagine how excited I was when I found that Art Nouveau wallpaper, patterned with irises, in a little antiques shop in Massachusetts. And then, at a Paris flea market, I saw those chairs that are so exquisitely connected to the wallpaper, with their silk upholstery printed with irises in the same pale blue and peach. ❧

The wainscoting is actually made of embossed wallpaper that was stained to look like wood. If you look in the mirror, you can see the reflection of the WC, which is shaped like a calla lily. It only came in white, but I had it reglazed in peach to go with the marble on the sink and the wallpaper. I love the heavy iridescent prisms on the Tiffany chandelier. The sconces are also by Tiffany.

GRANDMA'S HOUSE

When I first walked through the front door of this California ranch-style house, I couldn't believe that a home on the ocean could feel drab and dreary. Of course, it didn't help that the bushes and trees surrounding it were so overgrown you could barely see out the windows. Yet the place had charm, and I could see the potential. I didn't need to make it bigger, just better, and the idea was to work with what was already there.

I have no idea what that shelf is doing in the middle of the front door. Maybe it was going to be a Dutch door at one point. It was such a peculiar thing that I kept it. OPPOSITE: *The original house.*

When I bought this in 1994, I had just spent five years doing the Deco house and was in no mood for another major construction project. But what were they thinking, back in the 1950s when it was built? If you have a beautiful view like this, why would you put a closet with a big bulky oil heater right in front of it?

I couldn't wait to have that closet and some of the walls knocked down, to open up the space. The living room already had a nice rustic quality, with exposed rafters and a peaked ceiling—unfortunately painted a strange shade of green. But there was a bigger problem with that ceiling. One side of the peak was shorter than the other. The asymmetry made the whole room feel lopsided, so we moved a wall and built the short side out another three feet.

The aluminum sliding-glass doors had to go. (Those doors seem to be following me around. I've been stuck with them in every house I've redone.) We replaced them with French doors with built-in screens. The traditional paned glass—and a coat of white paint—changed the whole character of the space. Now it looked less 1950s and more like an old cottage on Cape Cod.

It felt fresh and clean, but still cozy, which was great because I planned to use it as a guesthouse. I kept the scale small and friendly, because I wanted to hold on to that intimacy. I'm just as comfortable in a small room as a large room . . . and the tinier bedrooms reminded me of the apartment where I grew up, back in Brooklyn.

I did the living room around an old Depression-era WPA sign I found in East Hampton. It was the inspiration for the red, white, and blue color scheme . . . very American . . . with a

TOP: *The living room as I first saw it. Right behind the hutch is the closet with the oil burner. Why did they need that dark hallway leading to the kitchen?* ABOVE: *It was so satisfying to open up the space. I wasn't sorry to see the oil burner go.* RIGHT: *Now French doors open to a brick terrace.* OPPOSITE: *I've always loved quilts, and I just tossed them over everything, very casually. To tell you the truth, I couldn't face looking for more fabric, and the quilts let me get away with a hodgepodge of furniture. The couch used to be in my dressing room in* The Mirror Has Two Faces *and the two club chairs were leftovers from* On a Clear Day You Can See Forever.

USA
WORK
PROGRAM
WPA

I'm always recycling things. I bought the red settee for the main house and moved it in here when it didn't work in there. The clowns on the table are from a circus set by Schoenhut, made at the turn of the last century.

little mustard thrown in for spice. Actually, the mustard came in because I took the mustard print curtains from the main house dining room and hung them in here. (They were very well made, and I would rather reuse something than throw it away.) I already had all the old painted furniture, which I had been collecting for years, storing it in a garage while it was waiting for a home. Now I finally had a place for all my hutches and cabinets. There's something so appealing about those old finishes . . . the layers of paint . . . and then the places where it's worn off so you can see the original wood underneath. I always wonder, Who lived with this piece? Who added the first layer of paint and then the second, as it was handed down through the years? In its way, it's just as beautiful to me as fine 18th-century mahogany. One style was for the poor people and the other was for the rich . . . and I've been both.

In the middle of the renovation, I decided to direct *The Mirror Has Two Faces*, which meant I had to move to New York for four months. I hired Tim Morrison to supervise the project (he helped during several trips) and I tried to keep on top of it through phone calls and Polaroids (no Internet back then). So I was decorating this house while I was talking to the set decorator about how I envisioned the apartment for Rose—the character I played in the movie. We only had four weeks of prep before we had to start shooting, and I realized I could save a lot of time by just using what I had already picked out for this house. The lace curtains I had chosen for the bedroom became Rose's lace curtains. And when we were picking out mirrors, light fixtures, and even the bathroom sink, I found myself choosing things that would work in both places. Then instead of tossing it all out when we finished shooting, I bought many of the pieces and shipped them back to this house. (Again, it's about reuse.)

LEFT, TOP: *The old painted hutch is filled with antique earthenware. I had the dining table made so I could get just the right oval shape.* LEFT, MIDDLE: *The little breakfast nook in the kitchen is furnished with an old table and painted chairs and a banquette that looks more like a sofa, with cushions and a skirt.* LEFT, BOTTOM: *I had to buy the O'Keefe & Merritt stove, which dates back to the 1950s, because it was the same mustard color as the original tiles in the kitchen.* OPPOSITE: *I put that wooden slice of watermelon on the cabinet because it looks as if it fell out of the painting.*

MUSTARD

What was it about that painting that appealed to me? The food. Food is always delectable to me, in any form and from any period.

I also ended up bringing in editing equipment and finishing the whole movie right here, in Grandma's house. My husband gave it that name, because he thought it looked like the house in the woods where Little Red Riding Hood's grandmother lived.

There's something very comforting about this house. I like to come over here to work. Most of the time, I'll have meetings here, especially with people I don't know, because it seems to put everyone at ease right away. There's nothing intimidating about it. People automatically relax.

I've even recorded many songs in here. The fact is, I'm lazy as well as energetic. I love my home and I don't like to leave it, and it's a long drive to the studios in Hollywood. So I set up my own system here. It's not exactly high-tech. I wheel my manicure table into the living room for the recording engineer and his computer, and then I go into the little lavender bedroom and sit on a stool, looking out at the ocean. The engineer sets up my mike, and I have my music stand for the lyrics and a little table for my tea. I put my earphones on and I sing. There are no special acoustics, not even double-glazed windows, but we're never bothered by the sound of the ocean. Go figure.

Then I'll go back to the living room and sit in that club chair with the deep yellow quilt and swivel around to listen to the playback from the two Genelec speakers on either side of the red settee. We installed a fiber-optic line, which means somebody could be mixing the album in London or Paris or Hollywood, but since we all have the same speakers, we all hear the same sound. I recorded my *Guilty Pleasures* album with Barry Gibb this way, and worked on *Higher Ground*, *A Love Like Ours*, *Christmas Memories*, *The Movie Album*, and *Love Is the Answer* in Grandma's house. Tony Bennett came over and we sang "Smile," our number on his *Duets* album, right here. I think Tony was a little bit shocked when he saw my "recording studio," but he was inspired enough to do a drawing of the view.

ABOVE: *The original fireplace needed a little help.* OPPOSITE: *I redid the stone and picked that large reddish rock for the center because it stood out amid all the others in the pile. It was unique and deserved a special place. The carved animals and dancing girls on the mantel are also from the Schoenhut circus. I love the simplicity of folk art and have collected it for years.*

TOP: *This bedroom doesn't look anything like a recording studio, but this is where I sing. It's my lavender recording booth. Lavender is my goddaughter Caleigh's favorite color. The chaise came from a former house, and I trimmed the new lavender pillows with antique lace.* MIDDLE, LEFT AND RIGHT: *My friend Maxine, who knew the story of how I used to pretend a hot water bottle was my doll, made this for me. You can turn the doll's head around to show either face—awake or asleep.* RIGHT: *I decided to knock out the bedroom ceilings, too. It gives you the sensation of more space, even though the perimeter of the room doesn't change.*

I covered everything with wallpaper, even the closet doors and the ceiling. I had the four-poster bed made out of pine, and found the crocheted canopy and matching coverlet on the Internet. The plaid taffeta curtains used to hang in the sitting room of the main house. Waste not, want not.

ABOVE: *Now it's the quintessential rose-covered cottage, but here's how it looked before.* FROM LEFT TO RIGHT: *The original garage, house, and driveway.*

And here's how it looks after. FROM LEFT: *Cobblestones you can drive on. An arched gate frames the cottage. The birdhouse that was hiding behind the porch post.*

Roses spill over the split-rail fence in the backyard. When I was growing up in Brooklyn, a view like this was the furthest thing from my mind. The ocean was Brighton Beach.

Red, white, and blue . . . and a touch of mustard. Those are the colors of the flowers around Grandma's house. If only I had the time and wasn't always dieting, we'd have afternoon tea under the trellis, a quiet, shady spot in the lathe house I drew up and Vicente built for me.

THE MAIN HOUSE

I love this house dearly. I love it, I love it, I love it because it didn't cause me any pain. I didn't have to pick out every molding and doorknob. Most of the places I've lived in required quite a lot of work, but this house needed very little. It was a gift.

It took me only three days to move everything in and it looked as if I'd been living here for years. All of my things just seemed to fit in this space. Remember, I waited 11 years to get this house, from the moment I first saw it in 1984 to the day I was able to buy it in 1995. I can't tell you how happy I felt when it was finally mine.

OPPOSITE: ***When people come to visit for the first time, I like to start at the main house and bring them through this front door. Then we'll walk through the gardens by Grandma's house on our way to the barn and the mill house, for the complete tour.***

The couple who renovated it did a very good job. I was so glad they had ripped off the modern gray horizontal siding on the exterior but I wasn't thrilled with the stone they chose to replace it. It looked too light and too new. Martha Stewart told me that if I brushed it with cow's urine and buttermilk it would turn darker. But we don't have cows, and buttermilk alone didn't work. So I planted Boston ivy (which I like because it changes with the seasons) and climbing roses to cover it up a bit.

I remembered the inside of the house as being quite charming in a cottagey sort of way, back when I first saw it in 1984. But I liked how the latest owners had dressed it up, adding columns and moldings and paneling and pilasters. The changes they made were basically what I would have done myself. It had an elegant formality, whereas Grandma's house is totally informal. I feel at home in both those settings. Grandma's house feels like the apartment I lived in as a child, with a tiny bathroom that the whole family shared. This house feels like it's for grown-ups.

And now I had the right setting for all the American furniture I had fallen in love with after my visits to Winterthur and the White House, Monticello, and Mount Vernon, and all those boat trips with stops in historic towns along the New England coast. Walking through those beautiful rooms from another century was so inspiring. I could see in my head how this house should look.

I had only one small regret. They had taken out the circular driveway, something I've never had and always wanted. Imagine the bliss . . . you could drive in and out without having to back out, hoping you don't hit the light fixtures. But it would have been a huge job to redo the driveway. So I'm still backing out. You can't have everything.

LEFT, FROM TOP: *To me, the stone looked too new. I thought it would be better with a soft blanket of Boston ivy, and I changed the garage doors to look like an old carriage house I saw on Martha's Vineyard. This is the view from the family room window before I redid the landscaping. I tore out the tall bushes so you could see the beautiful trunks of those old sycamores and the depth of the property, and planted burgundy marguerites and boxwood topiary balls.* OPPOSITE: *When you walk down the winding path to the front door, all the flowers are red because you're about to open the door to a room with lots of red upholstery.*

Above: The palette in the foyer was inspired by the American flag. I was lucky—the curtains were already there, and I had the Duncan Phyfe sofa reupholstered in the same red. The Sheraton chairs date back to 1800, and I was thrilled to see very similar chairs in a period room at the Metropolitan Museum of Art in New York. The end table on the right is attributed to Samuel McIntire. The folk art portraits are by Zedekiah Belknap.

The Foyer

When I first saw the house, it just had a modern glass overhang above the front door, and I remember thinking, This is not much of an entrance. So it was a godsend that the previous owners had already built a new foyer and I didn't have to do it. They even paneled the walls and added a pair of graceful arched niches. All I had to do was change the black and white marble floor, which I felt was a bit cold. I preferred wood. And I had windows cut into the front door to let in more light. But other than that, the room was great. Their architect had evidently measured properly, and the paneling lined up correctly. And I loved the hardware on the door, with its heavy brass rim lock and a nice old-fashioned key.

Since I wanted to furnish it in classic Federal style, I went to New York to see one of my favorite dealers, Albert Sack, who knows everything there is to know about American furniture. We marked off the dimensions of the foyer in his big showroom and started to move furniture around to see how various

ABOVE: *I used to have more furniture in the foyer, but I learned something as I was taking these photographs. It looked better with less, so I started pulling things out . . . 18th-century rooms were spare, and that's why they look so good. I bought the Tabriz rug at auction.* OPPOSITE, ABOVE: *The two folk art paintings on either side of the Duncan Phyfe table are by John Brewster Jr. I'm always drawn to mother-and-child portraits, and the mother happens to be wearing one of my favorite colors, that French blue-gray.* OPPOSITE, BELOW: *I always keep red flowers in this room.*

I love the look of paintings going up a staircase and have always hung them there ever since I had my first staircase in my apartment on Central Park West.

combinations would look. I picked out a Duncan Phyfe sofa that had pure, elegant lines, and Albert showed me a rare Queen Anne tea table, with pullout shelves for holding candlesticks, to go in front of it. I was attracted to the simpler pieces, and almost all of them turned out to be by Duncan Phyfe, including the mahogany table I chose to go against the opposite wall. I can't get over these things that were made such a long time ago and have survived all these years, with their beauty intact. The proportions are perfect. The craftsmanship is sublime. I feel privileged to be their caretaker for a while.

I didn't have to buy art for the walls, thanks to a particular passion that started back in 1985 when I happened to pass a room full of American folk art paintings on my way to a jewelry auction at Sotheby's. I had never really liked those flat, primitive paintings before (and I still don't like the ones where the children's faces look more like adults), but this was an exceptional collection. When I saw them, I thought, Oh my god, this is so beautiful. I fell in love with a painting of a mother, father, and four children and bid on it, shaking the whole time. I didn't even know who the artist was, and as the price climbed, I dropped out, only to see it go to the very next bidder. That made me even more determined to get the other one I liked, of a grandmother and child. It turned out to be by one of the masters of the genre, Ammi Phillips. At the same auction, I bought the two John Brewster Jr. portraits that are in this foyer.

The folk art seemed to suit this room, but I was still missing one element. I think the first thing you see as you walk in the door of a house is very important, and I wanted another painting . . . something to set the tone and celebrate America. I got very excited when I found out that a portrait of George Washington done by Charles Peale Polk was coming up for auction. It was especially interesting to me because it was painted in 1795, during Washington's lifetime. I couldn't get to New York to see it in person, so I asked a dealer I knew to check it out for me. Polk's depiction of Washington is very different from the Gilbert Stuart version on the dollar, and I find that fascinating. Which likeness is more accurate? We'll never know. But I did notice that the painting of George Washington that hangs in the White House looks more like mine. I lent the portrait to Mount Vernon for a while ... it felt nice to see Washington back in his house ... and it will eventually return there permanently.

OPPOSITE: *The fine 1735 Queen Anne wing chair next to the Duncan Phyfe card table was upholstered in traditional linsey-woolsey fabric, which I didn't want to remove, so I just had it slipcovered in navy blue velvet to pick up the color of George Washington's uniform in the Charles Peale Polk portrait. I thought of this as Washington's chair, so I had the pillow embroidered with his initials. The portraits along the stairs, starting at the top, are by Lydia Field Emmet, John Singer Sargent, and Robert Henri.*

The Living Room

It started with a pillow. Two throw pillows, to be exact, made from pieces of antique Aubusson in the most beautiful shade of faded apple green, with red and dark pink flowers. I must have bought them 30 years ago. They inspired the color scheme for this room, and then I saw an Aubusson rug in that same green, with roses, hanging in a shop window in London. I picked up the green in the curtains and chose 18th-century furniture for the room. It's funny . . . when I was filming *Funny Girl*, the set for Fanny Brice's house was filled with Chippendale furniture because she collected it, and I thought it was so stuffy. Now here I am, and my eye tells me it's gorgeous.

One day my friend Maxine came in and asked, "Do you ever sit here?" I had to admit that the two chaises upholstered in formal green damask by the fireplace weren't exactly cozy . . . and the couch in the bay window turned its back on the view. That's when I thought, Okay, I'll slipcover the chaises in a more casual flowery linen print and move them into the bay, which I added when I bought the house because the room needed a little interest. I also put a planter right outside the window so we could grow flowers in the same colors as the room. All of the flowers outside my rooms pick up the colors inside, because I feel the exteriors are an extension of the interiors, and they're all part of a whole. It makes the room look larger, too, to see the same colors outside.

TOP: *Martha and George Washington flank a circa 1750 Queen Anne highboy, along with two circa 1740 Queen Anne chairs that still have their original finish. I'm afraid to let anyone polish them in case it gets ruined, so they only get dusted. The portrait of a child is by Robert Henri.* ABOVE: *The pillow that inspired the living room. The flowers I planted outside pick up the same colors.* OPPOSITE: *I always put pink flowers in front of this portrait by John Singer Sargent, still in its original Stanford White frame.* PREVIOUS PAGES: *The circa 1770 Chippendale piecrust table also has its original finish. That's hard to imagine, after 240 years! It was once in the collection of Mr. and Mrs. Adolf Meyer, and Albert Sack convinced me I should have it in mine. After I bought the Chippendale chairs beside it, I sent them to Winterthur so the seats could be remade with horsehair in proper period fashion, and then covered in burgundy damask. The painting over the fireplace is by William McGregor Paxton. Only American artwork is hung in this room. Did you notice that all the women in the portraits are dressed in pink?*

Albert Sack advised me to buy this rare set of Chippendale chairs made in Philadelphia and signed by Samuel Walton, circa 1775. The sideboard happens to be 18th-century English . . . I'm still looking for a great American one. Above it is the painting that prompted the color scheme. I found the circa 1825 two-part corner cabinet in Maine.

The Dining Room

I've been collecting cranberry glass for years, buying pieces here and there in various antiques shops. They're not difficult to find and quite inexpensive . . . but so pretty.

I built the dining room around the painting by Georg Tappert that hangs over the sideboard. I bought it at auction in 1989, from the collection of the film director Billy Wilder. I thought it was gorgeous, like a German Expressionist Matisse. The burgundy color in the painting inspired the burgundy curtains, made from the same fine, satiny damask that I used on that pair of Chippendale chairs in the living room. When I bought the house, the dining room walls were done in a green wallpaper, and I only got around to changing it recently. By then the damask I had used for the curtains was discontinued, and I had to hunt high and low for something similar to use on the walls.

The dining table is English rather than American. English tables are less wide, which worked better in this room. Besides, I think it makes for better conversation when you're closer to the people on the opposite side. I needed more dining chairs and was thrilled to find a set of period Chippendale chairs at auction that happened to be upholstered in burgundy damask. Of course I had to buy them. It was as if they were meant for this room.

Thomas Hart Benton had such an original, distinctive style. He did this painting of Martha's Vineyard, where he spent many summers. OPPOSITE, BELOW: *The painting of Abraham Lincoln is also by Benton.* OPPOSITE, ABOVE: *There's always a place for children in my rooms. I've had the child-size Chippendale chairs for years, and dear Renata, who always finds the best presents, gave me the drop-leaf table to go with them.*

The Den

Originally this room was all knotty pine, with flowered curtains at the windows and too many tchotchkes. I didn't change it for 14 years, because I was so thrilled to have a wood-paneled den . . . but it looked like it had measles with all those spots. Finally, I couldn't stand it anymore and said to myself, I'm doing this over in three weeks. (I'm getting faster now, after spending five and a half years on the barn.)

I had a vision in my head. Twenty years ago, on one of my summer boat trips up the New England coast, we stopped in Newport, Rhode Island, and I walked through the historic Hunter House, a Georgian Colonial built in 1748. The den had olive green paneling and burgundy damask on the furniture—just one fabric everywhere, which looks so simple and refined. That room stayed in my brain all these years.

It took awhile to get the right olive green. We used milk paint, like they did in the 18th century, and my expert painter, Richard Davis, kept mixing different shades, trying to match a certain green in the Aubusson carpet I found at Mansour. He painted samples for me on large pieces of cardboard, and we looked at them in various lights. I wanted a quiet color . . . muted . . . and then I had another idea. What if we highlighted a few details in gold? As in the Schönbrunn Palace Jim and I visited while I was on my European concert tour. They actually put gold trim on mahogany as well, which I had never seen before . . . and plan to do one day.

Here, it would have to be very subtle, almost as if the sunlight had just picked out the classic fluted lines of a Corinthian pilaster . . .

ABOVE: *The knotty pine den looked like this for years until I finally had had enough of those knots.* LEFT: *I had never forgotten this room in the Hunter House and used a more muted version of the olive green and the burgundy.* OPPOSITE: *When I redid the room, I also masked the asymmetry by making a paneled cover for the French doors to the left of the fireplace, to match the doors on the right (which hide the TV). The painting above the mantel is by Ammi Phillips.*

The HIRSHHORN
MUSEUM & SCULPTURE GARDEN
VICTORIAN AMERICA
AMERICAN ART
WORLD WAR II

or the acanthus leaves on a capital. And guess what? Frank and Dean Levy, New York dealers and the sons of Bernard Levy, who had found many great pieces of antique American furniture for me, told me that they used to do that in America, too, back in the 18th century. I didn't know that. I just did it because I thought the touch of gold . . . the right gold, of course (when you squint you don't even see it, because it's the same tone as the paint . . . not too bright), would be beautiful against the dull olive green.

The black marble around the fireplace was also starting to bother me

LEFT: *Look at the detail on this tassel. We had a hard time finding it. I was told there was no tassel to match the fringe. I said, That's impossible. Whoever made the fringe has that thread. I got on the phone myself, and of course they had a tassel, and it's beautiful.* ABOVE, LEFT: *Richard LaGravenese and I sat face-to-face at that partners desk and didn't get up until the script for* The Mirror Has Two Faces *was finished.* ABOVE, RIGHT: *It was a challenge to find books I actually wanted that were bound in either burgundy or olive.* OPPOSITE, ABOVE: *For years I kept my awards tucked away in an office where no one could see them. Then when I redid this room, I thought, It's okay to bring them out. And besides, they go with the gold trim.* OPPOSITE, BELOW: *The trim is done in that rich, old gold leaf. Nothing else has that soft luster.* PREVIOUS PAGES: *The felt on the circa 1740 Queen Anne card table is now burgundy to suit the room. That's a very early alarm clock on top of it. The portrait over the sofa is by Ammi Phillips.*

because I thought the white veining made it look too busy. I went to several stone yards and found marble in my shade of olive green. I was ready to buy it and then I thought, Nope. It won't look right. There will be no demarcation between the wood and the fireplace if they're both in the same green. And digging out the old marble would ruin the woodwork. Better to leave it there. But then I thought my painter might be able to do a faux marble on top of it in burgundy. That didn't work. The veining never looked quite right. So I left it black, which actually picks up the clothing in the two Ammi Phillips portraits in the room.

I know I'm breaking the rules with that couch, which is not exactly period, but I wanted a comfortable place to sit or lie down, as my husband likes to do when he watches TV. (It's very difficult to lie down on an antique sofa.) Actually, this is the couch we used backstage during my concert tour. I just had it recovered in a Merlot-colored velvet. The striped fabric on the lolling chairs is something I found years ago, but I only had enough to do the fronts and had to use something else on the backs. Recently I bought the Queen Anne card table from the Levy brothers in New York. It was lined in bright green felt, but I'm such a nut . . . I could never live with that bright green. Luckily, the felt was old, but not original, so I had it redone in burgundy felt. Much better.

The furniture is all covered in one fabric, a warm wheat-colored chenille. The one exception is the child's chair, upholstered in its original rose-colored velvet.

The Family Room

This is where we hang out. It's the coziest room in the house, with big, comfortable couches and plenty of ottomans to put your feet up. We'll watch TV or a movie in here on a screen (hidden in a hollow beam) that slides down in front of the French doors. Sometimes we'll eat in front of the TV, on two little tables that Vicente made for us. It's so easy to live with this kind of simple pine furniture. If you put a glass down and it leaves a ring, it just adds character. You can relax around it in a way you can't around 18th-century mahogany. I'll sit here with my laptop and work while Jim is nearby on his. We both love massages, and sometimes we'll have them late at night in front of the fire.

LEFT: *A Thomas Hart Benton painting hangs on the left in the hallway, which leads to the family room.* ABOVE: *There's definitely a food theme going on in and around this turn-of-the-last-century American hutch. All the paintings depict food, and the miniature grocery shops underneath, from France and Germany, are selling good things to eat.* OPPOSITE: *Vintage Raggedy Ann dolls are tucked under an American secretary I use to display more doll furniture.* PREVIOUS PAGES: *I love those wicker chairs because the weave is so open. You can always see the fire through them. I found most of the old fireplace utensils at auctions . . . a bed warmer you filled with coals . . . an iron pot . . . a teapot on a stand. The painting on the mantel was done on a pine panel back around 1779. That little Tiffany lamp with apple blossoms and a mosaic base was the only one I kept when I sold my collection.*

I was so happy to finally have a place for all those things that had been stashed in the garage at the ranch for years. I found that kitchen table back in the 1980s at the Pier Show in New York. It was old and worn and had a lazy Susan built right into the pine top. Practical.

I picked up most of the old wooden signs at flea markets out in the Hamptons. Now they're hanging in the flower room, which used to be a laundry room with a washer, dryer, and an extra refrigerator thrown in. I would have loved to have kept the refrigerator for flower bulbs, but we actually use it for extra food. There's a big farm table where we can arrange flowers, a deep sink, and dozens of different vases to choose from. In my former house we used to do flowers in the kitchen but it was a mess—we would wind up with petals in the chicken soup. To have one space exclusively for flower arranging is a real treat.

But a space for cars is another thing. Each house has a garage, and yet our cars are still out in the driveway because the garages are being used for other things, like outdoor furniture for my yearly dog party and suitcases and the sewing machine I bought when I was 19 (which we still use for repairs). And where else are you going to put all those paper towels you bought at Costco?

ABOVE: *The lazy Susan in the center of the table is great, especially for Chinese food.* RIGHT: *Here's my old garage, filled with furniture, including that table and the Windsor chairs, with beautiful flowers painted on top.* OPPOSITE: *The farm table in the flower room was my dining table back in the 1970s. I thought those wooden children with their watering cans were too pretty to be stuck in the ground outside . . . with the cars, which are now slowly rusting in the salt air.*

TOMATOES
BACON
LETTUCE
VEGETABLES
STRAWBERRIES
KFAST
LUNCHEON
GLADS
FRESH EGGS

The Bedrooms

My bedroom is the color of vanilla ice cream . . . a soft ivory white. Everything is all one color, which makes the room seem quiet and serene. Of course, what you don't see is the stack of books by the bed . . . and the papers . . . and the telephone . . . and the laptop . . . and the TV. Jim and Sammie and I spend a lot of time in this room. In the mornings, we like to stay in bed for a bit . . . read . . . write . . . check out the news. It's peaceful up here in our little cocoon.

There was no paneling in this room when I moved in. The walls were completely plain, which didn't seem to go with the rest of the house. And the room was an odd shape, with a low alcove along one wall. I decided to build out that wall to square off the space. Then I could panel the whole suite and make the new wall the focal point, with a fireplace in the center. (I never cease to be thrilled when I see a fireplace in a bedroom. My first grown-up apartment on Central Park West had one, and I was in heaven.) Arched glass-fronted cabinets on either side hold interesting things . . . of which I have way too many. Before any of this was finished, I had to leave for New York to direct *The Mirror Has Two Faces*. Building the Deco house had been such an ordeal that I was very happy to be far, far away during the construction.

When I came back, it was all done. The Adam fireplace was superb. The moldings were beautiful. But the muntins on the glass doors of the cabinets were an inch thick, instead of the five-eighths of an inch I had specified. Now, I realize the difference doesn't sound like much, but the thicker muntins looked clunky and threw off the proportions. Besides that, they had used Plexiglas instead of real glass. Yet I just couldn't face taking off the doors and having them remade at the time. So I lived with them for years, until I went off for my 2007 concert tour and had them redone while I was in Europe. Now the muntins are just five-eighths of an inch thick . . . and delicate, as they would have been in the 18th century. And the glass is old-fashioned and wavy . . . and I'm happy.

I had the furniture shop at Warner Bros. make the mahogany canopy for me. Then I looked through my collection of antique lace and picked out a few pieces and draped them up there with the help of Renata. We stood on the bed and just tacked them up. The portrait is by Mary Cassatt, who was so good at depicting children, and the antique baby dolls echo the picture. By the way, the bed is made up like this only when company's coming. Most of the week it's what we call "bed ready," with simple, comfortable sheets and pillows. Sammie and I come up here in the late afternoon, because this is where she likes to have her nap.

I wanted subtle cream-on-cream detailing on the bedroom wall . . . and scalloped muntins on the fanlights. LEFT, TOP TO BOTTOM: *When I first saw this room, there were two beds in an alcove. I decided to build a wall with a fireplace. It's flanked by built-in cabinets. They're filled with various mementos, like these tortoiseshell accessories. A French doll sits amid a collection of creamware, which I've always loved. My son, Jason, did that little drawing when he was still in his teens, then had it reproduced by a jeweller for me as a surprise. (But I still prefer the original on the right.) Jason has great taste and is a great joy.*

This is my sitting room, but it's also my workroom. Now you know why the barn looks so pristine . . . this is where I really live. I have two desks in here. I used to use the one in front for trading stocks. Some mornings I still get up very early and see what the market is doing, and then start trading. I've been doing this for so long that it feels like another career.

I didn't clean up the room for this photo. (I haven't even changed the flowers yet, after the weekend.) There are books on the desks, books on the floor, and the piles of papers get very high, especially when I'm in the midst of a project like this book . . . or a new album. My trading desk is currently laden with photographs I've taken for this book. The other desk is for my day-to-day life—notes, bills, and auction catalogues, which I like to follow, even though I don't buy much anymore. I've run out of space.

LEFT: *The roses pick up the colors of the room.* ABOVE: *I like the seashell detailing in the arched niches. The white cabinet underneath the one on the right was made for me by Vicente and sized to fit the layouts for this book . . . in all its various versions.* OPPOSITE: *As you can see, I've managed to fill every available surface with family photographs. I like a small, cozy chair . . . it holds you tight.*

ABOVE: *I turned one bedroom into a gym, although there are more tchotchkes in here than exercise equipment. The only reason I exercise at all is because of Gaylene Ray, who has been my trainer for more than 30 years. I love seeing her sweet face three times a week.* CLOCKWISE, FROM TOP: *Roses match the doll's costume. I like the real fern in front of the fern in the painting. Here's a collection of old-fashioned hair stuff.* OPPOSITE: *That's my long-faced doll on the left. She's modeled after the Jumeau Triste (with a sad face) and rare because only a few were made. My doll buddy Michael Canadas dressed her. I'd love that coat myself.*

Molly's Room

I did this room over for Molly, Jim's daughter, when she was a teenager. I saw this old-fashioned wallpaper in London, with all those subtle blue-greens I've always been drawn to. Then I found the white cane furniture from the 1920s in East Hampton, at one of those outdoor antiques shows. I had the mirror over the beds made to go with the furniture. It was supposed to be bigger . . . but we won't go into that. The costume in the corner is the one I wore on the cover of *George* magazine, when John F. Kennedy, Jr. asked me to pose as Betsy Ross. I asked if they could make the dress in the same blue taffeta as the curtains, because I thought the costume would look good here. And the antique dolls just seemed to belong, because they're dressed in the same colors as the wallpaper. ❧

Epilogue

Why do I search for beauty? The world was always a strange place for me as a child and as a teenager who was told I couldn't be what I wanted to be . . . and now as an adult experiencing these complicated and dangerous times . . . man's cruelty to man . . . wars . . . the planet being destroyed by reckless, uncaring polluters.

I long for beauty and things you can count on...like the first bloom on my roses after they've been asleep for three months . . . a wooden floor with the imprint of time in its well-worn dents . . . the moonlight reflected on the ocean . . . a green egg.

And then there's the personal . . . love . . . kindness . . . friendships . . . being of service . . . giving back. I cherish the look on a face that tells you you've touched someone's life . . . that you made a difference.

I'm very grateful for all that has been given to me.

The other evening I was sitting in my dressing room before going out, when my eye was caught by the beauty of the sky. The cloud formations were spectacular, in the most delicate shades of peachy pink. I immediately thought, I've got to go get my camera. And then I realized . . . the book is done. I no longer have to document everything I see. All that's left to do now is to be in the moment . . . and enjoy it. ❧

Acknowledgments

The people who have helped me the most are already mentioned by name in the pages of this book, but there are others I would like to thank as well.

The staff of Viking—Clare Ferraro, for believing I could finish this book in time for Christmas. Executive Editor Rick Kot, for his constantly encouraging words. He made the experience a delight with his taste and his wit. And Fabiana Van Arsdell, for going to Spain to watch the book come off the presses and make sure the colors were right. I'd also like to thank my attorney, Robert Barnett, who made it happen.

Doug Turshen, my art director, has been working on this book with me for two years. I've been taking pictures for about seven. That means he's had to deal with 52,824 photographs. Thank you, Doug, for your patience, fortitude, and talent . . . and for executing every little change I asked for in the layouts. And to Steve Turner, for assisting admirably in that task. I couldn't have done it without you both.

I'd like to thank those photographers who helped me with things I really couldn't do . . . like use lights. Dear Edward Addeo, for showing me what a real photographer is like and giving me one of his golden reflectors. Peter Vitale, who taught me a few techniques (which I immediately forgot). Russell James, whom my pal Donna Karan brought over on my birthday to take a picture of me. It was serendipitous, because I was missing that last picture by the main house door. And Firooz Zahedi, who really knows about lighting and has been photographing me for years.

I want to thank my assistants on this project—Kim Skalecki, always; sweet Stefanie Sowa; then Bernadette Stewart, with her energetic spirit, who managed to do many things well; and Karen Swenson, who had the difficult task of finding pictures without a professional system.

John Johannessen, my brother-in-law/contractor . . . even though we had some difficult times, you never ran away. And others who helped him—Ceci Clarke, George Peper, Rick Holz, Danny del Do, Sten Miles, Craig George, Bob Newlon, Jamie Harnish, and John's wife, Bobbie, my sister-in-law.

My good buddy Maxine Smith, who also loves the hunt. Joe Rizzo, who sent me extra beams when I needed them. Billy Avila, the fastest upholsterer I've ever met. Jim Dummit, Jose Lujvidin,

Gary Perlberg, Paul McGrane. Elias Mendoza, a great carpenter. Brian Bell. Caesar Medina, Peter McWilliams, Albert Elihu. Gerardo Troncoso and Anthony Chaves for my beautiful stone. Deborah Wald, Scott Mitchell, Peter Fletcher, Rick Jagerson, Rob Shattuck, Jim Betts, Lynn Rutter, Morris Sheppard, Carolyn Brenton, Brent Hull, Ofer Abutbul, Mike Mullen, Miguel Morales. The lovely tile vendors. Nick Fortune, again, thanks for all my goodies. Landscapers Sam Maphis, who started the drawings years ago and Dennis Turner, who finished them.

And to all of you who think you should have been mentioned (especially architects), I still appreciate you.

There are certain people I can't thank enough.

Renata Buser, who takes such good care of me. She was always there to hand me my food and hand me my camera, like a doctor's assistant with a scalpel, and printed out my pictures day and night, seven days a week sometimes.

Vicente Viera and Javier Cansino, "my guys." Whenever I asked, "Can you do that?" they always said, "No problem." Love those words!

Marty Erlichman, who has been my representative since I was 19 years old. There's always a reason to thank him.

Samantha, my furry little girl who never takes a bad picture, as you can tell from this book.

My husband, Jim Brolin. Thank you for allowing me my obsession . . . and for listening and looking and researching and driving and drawing and loving the process, too.

And last but not least, Christine Pittel, who has my deepest gratitude for giving me love and support and encouraging me to keep writing, even though it was painful at times. I couldn't ask for a better editor. We were always on the same wavelength . . . wanting it to be the best it could be. Loving the quiet, we would talk in the wee small hours of the morning, like two nitpicking night owls, about everything from architecture to food to our love of chickens . . . and never get bored. What I'll remember most about this experience is making a precious new friend.

Where's the TV?

FROM LEFT: *In the Federal lounge, page 132, a flat-screen TV rises from an antique chest. In the master bath in the barn, page 178, it's hidden in an antique sewing table. In the Greene & Greene library, page 152, it's behind the cabinet doors over the fireplace.*

Photography Credits

Principal Photography by Barbra Streisand
Additional Photography By Edward Addeo, Peter Vitale, Firooz Zahedi

Page 20: Philippe Halsman, Magnum Photos / © New York Daily News, L.P. used with permission; Howell Conant / *Look* Magazine; Richard Champion/ *Architectural Digest*. Copyright © Condé Nast

Page 21: Bill Helms / House Beautiful; John Vaughan / Architectural Digest. Copyright © Condé Nast; John Vaughan / INSTYLE® used by permission of Time Inc.

Page 26: The Monticello Tea Room photographs are reprinted with permission from Monticello/Thomas Jefferson Foundation, Inc., and the photographer Laurence Bartone.

Page 116, 218, and 295: "FUNNY GIRL" © 1968, renewed 1996 Columbia Pictures Industries, Inc.,
All Rights Reserved, Courtesy of Columbia Pictures

Page 138: Excerpt from "Anthem" by Leonard Cohen. Copyright 1992 Sony/ATV Music Publishing LLC. All rights administered by Sony/ATV Music Publishing LLC, 8 Music Square West, Nashville, TN 37203. All rights reserved. Used by permission.

Page 295: "THE MIRROR HAS TWO FACES" © 1996 TriStar Pictures, Inc.
All Rights Reserved, Courtesy of TriStar Pictures /
"THE PRINCE OF TIDES" © 1991
Columbia Pictures Industries, Inc.
All Rights Reserved, Courtesy of Columbia Pictures

VIKING
Published by the Penguin Group
Penguin Group (USA) Inc., 375 Hudson Street,
New York, New York 10014, U.S.A.
Penguin Group (Canada), 90 Eglinton Avenue East, Suite 700,
Toronto, Ontario, Canada M4P 2Y3
(a division of Pearson Penguin Canada Inc.)
Penguin Books Ltd, 80 Strand, London WC2R 0RL,
England
Penguin Ireland, 25 St. Stephen's Green, Dublin 2, Ireland
(a division of Penguin Books Ltd)
Penguin Books Australia Ltd, 250 Camberwell Road,
Camberwell,
Victoria 3124, Australia
(a division of Pearson Australia Group Pty Ltd)
Penguin Books India Pvt Ltd, 11 Community Centre,
Panchsheel Park,
New Delhi – 110 017, India
Penguin Group (NZ), 67 Apollo Drive, Rosedale, North
Shore 0632,
New Zealand (a division of Pearson New Zealand Ltd)
Penguin Books (South Africa) (Pty) Ltd, 24 Sturdee Avenue,
Rosebank, Johannesburg 2196, South Africa

Penguin Books Ltd, Registered Offices:
80 Strand, London WC2R 0RL, England

First published in 2010 by Viking Penguin,
a member of Penguin Group (USA) Inc.

1 2 3 4 5 6 7 8 9 10

ISBN 978-0-670-02213-7

Printed in Spain
Set in Requiem
Designed by Doug Turshen with Steve Turner

A portion of the proceeds from this book will be donated to the Barbra Streisand Women's Cardiovascular Research and Education Program at Cedars-Sinai Medical Center.

BARBRA STREISAND

ridge
Beam
color

lite
FIXTures
(doors)
French
fixTure?
ok

from ...
Lounge door

John +
B.B 3) Lounge paneling - window seat -
Danny O. see Jacks drawing again + make a panel
of one   single panel
some of panel
is hidden

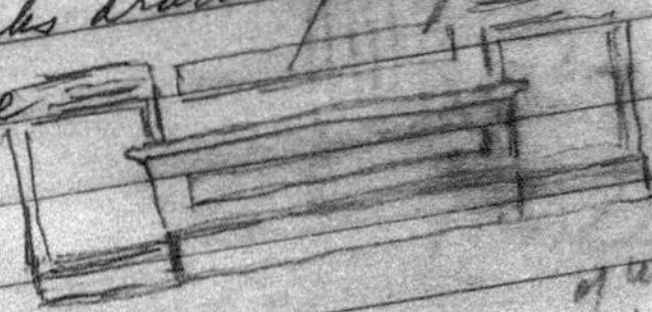

4) how do u finish edge of wall w/o casing down to
chairail?

5) Can B.P touch up MTF posts + ...
... gym

... in silo Bath - co...

... fabrics + Trims fo...
...ings - I Put away ...

To get at
Home Depot
1) Glidden paint
Classic + Neutral
"BARRISTER White"
30YY 80/088
low Sheen Pearl? or Satin eggshell?

2) BEHR Premium plus
NAVAJO WHITE
1822
(top of card it says W-D-320)

MAY 6th 2007
1) order Mecca Rug Voysey for ...
shades of rose + browns (Bern pic...
Dennis 2) GRASS Down on Ocean side
to Keep area clean -
3) Curtains on ocean side to Keep
from fading - Library, Kitch...
Great Rm?
4) order Blinds for office - frank

... price can't be $159 a ya...

...Lounge - No crown in MACK/sheh...

... copper vase ...
5) Kim - (redirect all E Ma...
6) H - what ... applian...
exactly (2 frig drawers
do we have - any mista...
7) Tim Before sunrise I wa...
the colors of the sk...
from at bottom a ...
peachy color to dele...
to blue - later ...
yellow at bottom ...
yellow (ombreéd) ...
color that looks ...

Folding Back with
panels with
Looks behind
shutters

3'16"